JACKASSES OF HISTORY

Bathroom Reader

& Handy Manual of Unpleasant Trivia

By Seann McAnally

PHARAOH PUBLISHING USA

For Conley Stone McAnally
My Dad

CONTENTS

INTRODUCTION

For some reason, exactly 24 weeks ago, I made a blog entry about Thomas Seymour and what a douchebag he was. A few people "liked" it on social media. So I did another one. A few more people "liked" it. Addicted to "likes," I kept writing more, for about 20 straight weeks, until I got burned out. Hence this book.

I should take a moment to clarify that I'm not a historian. I'm more of a storyteller. It's not my job to give the reader a completely unbiased view of these jackasses. Some of them, like General George B. McClellan, have their share of admirers. Truth be told, there are some good qualities in every jackass.

So don't take anything you read in this book as gospel truth. I've read at least one book or lengthy article on each of these jackasses, and supplemented with material from the dreaded internet. Bottom line is, I've not even attempted to give any of these jackasses the "fair shake" that a trained, ethical historian might give them.

We can argue over the definition of a jackass. Some of the people in this book are incompetent. Some of them are well-intentioned but had poor judgment. Others were just plain evil. Why do they deserve a spotlight?

PHA020 • ISBN 978-0692538098

Issued under exclusive license to
Pharaoh Publishing USA
www.pharaohpublishingusa.com

Cover collage by Seann McAnally
Cover and interior images from the public domain

Let's face it, everyone loves—or loves to hate—a jackass. The folly of someone like the Earl of Bothwell makes us feel better about our own mistakes. When we struggle with our own anger management issues, we can always take comfort that we're doing better than Mussolini. And if we ever fantasize about murdering someone, we'll know how not to lose the murder weapon (ahem, John Thurtell) or not to hand the cops a damning clue on a silver platter (lookin' at you, Harvey Hawley Crippen).

We venerate the heroes of history, and rightly so. But in the final analysis, it's always the flawed heroes like Francis Drake or Alexander the Great who are the most interesting. Maybe vices are more interesting than virtues. After all, there are no TV crime documentaries about people who chose *not* to rape and murder someone.

If bogeys are more interesting than boons, then collected here are 20 of the most interesting people you'll ever meet—deeply flawed, disturbed, selfish, arrogant, malicious, homicidal, or just plain dumb, these men and women are likely to make you feel better about yourself.

So turn the page and prepare to feel superior to the Jackasses of History. I hope you enjoy it.

Seann McAnally
Kansas City, Missouri
September 2015

Our first jackass was a power-hungry, princess-molesting, would-be ruler who thought he'd kidnap and control a young king. Instead, he wound up with his head on a chopping block.

THOMAS SEYMOUR

Thomas Seymour is our first Jackass of History. By all accounts, Seymour was courageous and good-looking. He was also vain, jealous, and, to make matters worse, incompetent. Had he managed himself better, he could have been one of the most powerful men in England. Instead, he was executed for treason.

Said Nicholas Throckmorton, a friend of King Edward VI, of Seymour: "hardy, wise and liberal...fierce in courage, courtly in fashion, in personage stately, in voice magnificent, but somewhat empty of matter."

Seymour's sister Jane caught the eye of King Henry VIII as his relationship with Ann Boleyn fell apart, primarily due to her inability to give him a male heir. He married Jane 11 days after Ann's execution. Henry seems to have truly loved Jane, at least insofar as he was capable. She gave him his long-awaited male heir, Prince Edward (the future King Edward VI). Unfortunately, she died from complications of childbirth some two weeks later. Both of Jane's brothers were given powerful positions at court. The elder brother, Edward, was the more responsible and capable of the two, and was one of Henry's privy councilors. Thomas was never granted a councilorship by Henry, who seems to have realized he was a jackass.

Like a lot of good-looking jackasses, he managed to

capture the attention of an otherwise lovely, respectable, and classy lady, Catherine Parr, whose attraction to Seymour seems to have been her only major flaw. She was one of the richest widows in England. They began a flirtation that was a great frustration to her friends and advisers. Seymour—either because he loved her or because of her fortune—proposed marriage. Unfortunately, Henry VIII had also noticed Catherine and proposed marriage. As a religious reformer, she felt God had called her to this position. Henry had been backsliding toward Catholicism ever since his break with Rome. She hoped to continue to sway him toward more radical Protestant reform, and even got herself into trouble a few times over it (fascinating tales that must be told elsewhere). With a heavy heart, she rejected Seymour's proposal and accepted Henry's.

Henry then sent Seymour to the continent to manage some parts of his disastrous and costly military campaigns in France. Seymour's bravery meant he met with a few successes, capturing two castles under the command of Sir John Wallop (pack a Wallop?). Otherwise, he was not particularly successful, failing in an important mission to recruit German mercenaries to serve Henry.

Returning to England shortly before Henry's death, Seymour was miffed that he was not on the Privy Council, and resentful that his brother Edward was high in the king's favor. He was determined to weasel his way into the royal family, expressing an interest in marrying either of Henry's daughters (Mary and Elizabeth). Nothing came of this, which surprised no one but Seymour.

Then Henry died, leaving Seymour's older brother Edward as "Lord Protector" for the child King Edward

VI. Seymour was made a privy councilor, but this
did not satisfy his ambition. He was given a few titles
and appointments as a sort of consolation prize.
Nevertheless, Thomas was consumed with jealousy of
his older brother and constantly sought to undermine
his influence over the young king.

Henry's death left Catherine Parr vast wealth and
the freedom to marry again. Seymour swooped in and
the two were married secretly, quite soon after the
king's death. Seymour and Parr moved to his estates
in the country. They were made protectors of Princess
Elizabeth, who Seymour liked. A lot. When she was
14 years old, he began deeply inappropriate behavior
toward her that probably amounted to full-on sexual
abuse. However, it is unknown to what degree Elizabeth
may or may not have been victimized. A strong-willed
young lady faced with attention from a good-looking
man, she may not have put up much resistance. All that
was acknowledged publicly was that he would "romp"
with her, tickle her, "slappe her behinde as she lay abed"
and other things. It is even said Parr joined in a few of
these "romps." Whatever happened between them, when
Parr became pregnant by Seymour (her first child),
she became deeply concerned over his behavior with
Elizabeth and sent her away to live elsewhere. But then
Parr herself died, and Seymour attempted to reconnect
with Elizabeth. Already quite astute despite her years,
Elizabeth took great pains to avoid him (this lends
credence to the belief that she was a victim of sexual
abuse, not a willing partner in their "romps").

Frustrated in his attempt to marry Elizabeth, Seymour
began to secretly exercise influence over the young
King Edward, using his vast wealth to give the king a
generous allowance. The king was utterly reliant on

others for pocket money, and this enabled him to give gifts and feel more king-like and adult. Seymour tried to cajole Edward into making him his personal governor, but this came to nothing. Finally, Seymour openly attempted to persuade the king to curtail his brother's power, which, again, came to naught. The young King Edward, in fact, seems to have held little respect for either of his Seymour uncles, preferring instead the counsel of Catherine Parr's brother, who he referred to tellingly as his "honest uncle" to distinguish him from the Seymours.

Seymour became increasingly more vocal in criticizing his elder brother and calling his policies into question. Seymour was the nominal "lord admiral" of the British fleet, whom he unwisely tried to enroll in a possible rebellion. Failing this, he negotiated with pirates on the western coasts who it was his job to keep at bay. All of this became too suspicious, and the privy council moved to order his arrest. But, despite being treated shamefully by his little brother, Edward Seymour, the Lord Protector, called a council so that Thomas could try to explain himself. This would have probably saved his life, but he never showed up to the hearing.

Soon after, in a staggering display of jackassery, Seymour, perhaps slightly unhinged, attempted to sneak into King Edward's bedchambers. We'll never know why, but it was considered most likely at the time that he was attempting to spirit the young king away, so that he could physically control the royal person and make a bid for power. Like the jackass he was, Seymour failed to realize or remember that the king routinely slept with several dogs. A spaniel barked at Seymour and he shot it. He was suddenly surrounded by palace guards, and being caught outside the king's bedchamber with a loaded gun was too much to explain away. There was no longer anything his big brother could do for him—Seymour was arrested the next day and charged with 33 counts of treason. He was executed within the month, his estates and wealth confiscated by the crown, and his daughter Mary left a destitute orphan.

A byproduct of all this is that the great men of the realm came to know Elizabeth first-hand. All of Seymour's associates were ruthlessly questioned, including Elizabeth, to see who was complicit in his treason. Although she was not *first* in line to succeed Edward if he died, she was in line, and her association with Seymour placed her under suspicion. During relentless questioning, the sordid details of Seymour's guardianship of her came to light, though Elizabeth is believed to have downplayed this to avoid embarrassment. During her questioning, the council was reportedly impressed with her poise, personal magnetism, and "polite defiance." She was removed from all suspicion, and made a few contacts who would serve her well when she did become queen.

So, for not realizing his own limitations, for his inability to be content with the incredible good fortune that repeatedly fell into his lap, for molesting a 14-year-old princess, for being stupid enough to think he could foment rebellion, and for grossly bungling his attempt to kidnap the young king, Seymour is, indeed, a true Jackass of History.

Unpleasant Trivia...

• Between 1890 and 1910, Bayer's Heroin was available in nearly every corner drugstore. It was advertised as a non-addictive substitute for morphine. Among its other reputed properties was that it could cure coughing in children.

He terrorized both criminals and law-abiding citizens in a dangerous game of good cop/bad cop. As things turned out, he couldn't have it both ways—and paid the ultimate price.

JONATHAN WILD

Jonathan Wild was both cop and criminal. He may not rank as a *complete* "jackass of history" because he was (arguably) competent until the end of his career. But Wild, the so-called "Thief-Taker General" of London, is an interesting character nonetheless, and approaches jackassery close enough to be included in our Jackasses of History.

Wild was born in the late 1600s to a carpenter. As a young man he was an apprentice buckle-maker in Wolverhampton but left for London to work as a servant. He was soon fired from this job, returned to Wolverhampton, then shortly thereafter left his wife and child to return to London. He soon found himself in debtor's prison, but made himself popular by running errands for the guards. He was able to scrape together enough to buy his freedom. In prison he met a prostitute named Molly, who got him involved with her gang of thieves and whores. He became an expert in the underworld, serving as a pimp and a fence. He lived with Molly as her husband, even though both were already married, and served as her pimp.

Wild eventually got a job as a deputy for notoriously corrupt "Under-Marshall" Charles Hitchen, who routinely extorted money and goods, enriching himself in his position. Unfortunately this was normal at

the time. London had no effective police force and
a population of about 70,000—huge for the early
1700s—and crime was on the rise. London was crawling
with unemployed soldiers after the War of the Spanish
Succession, which made matters worse. Wild served
under Hitchen, but continued to fence goods and act as
a pimp for Molly and several other prostitutes.

Eventually, Wild realized he could do better on his
own—away from both Molly and Hitchen. Like a true
jackass, he cut off Molly's ear to mark her as a prostitute.
He set up an office, called himself Hitchen's "deputy"
even though he wasn't, and wore a sword despite the
fact that he did not have "gentleman" status (which was
illegal).

Nevertheless, the city's fear of crime allowed him to
operate as a thief-taker. He became wildly popular as
he appeared to be successful at curbing crime (he sent
some 60 thieves to the gallows). In truth, he specialized
in having items stolen, waiting for the theft to be
reported, then "discovering" the goods and returning
them for a reward. If a scapegoat was needed, Wild
would offer up a member of a rival gang or one of his
own gang members who had crossed him. He fenced
goods for them and kept the majority of profits for
himself, amassing a decent pile of wealth. If he came
into possession of stolen goods that would allow him
to blackmail someone—such as finding a personal
belonging in a whorehouse—he would often put out
an advertisement in one of the many news-sheets of
London, with the blackmail implied.

He became so popular that the Privy Council that
advised the king asked for his input on new ways of
controlling crime. Near-jackass that he was, Wild
advised that the reward for capturing a thief be increased

by 300 percent. Obviously, this was to his benefit and he continued to enrich himself.

When he'd tackle another gang, he would make sure the news-sheets knew about his heroics. But while appearing to be acting for the public good, Wild was just engaging in gang wars disguised as law enforcement. He soon controlled London's largest crime ring, one of the first we can consider "organized crime" in the modern sense.

Things began to go badly when he tangled with a former associate who had struck out on his own—Jack Sheppard. He was handsome, well-liked, and seen as something of a Robin Hood-type by the apprentices and cockney folk of London. He was also known for non-violence, which was probably the cause of his falling-out with Wild in the first place. Wild had him arrested, but he escaped. He was arrested again, and escaped. The news-sheets had a field day with this. Eventually Wild got Sheppard's wife so drunk she betrayed his secrets, and he was arrested again—and escaped again. This made Wild look bad in the press, and Sheppard's supporters began to grumble about Wild's apparent (and actual) hypocrisy.

West arrested a partner of Sheppard's named Blake. At trial, Blake begged to be transported to the colonies instead of facing execution, but Wild blocked the request. In a rage, Blake managed to launch himself at Wild and slit his throat. He survived, but was laid low for quite some time. Blake was executed.

Meanwhile, Sheppard was captured again, wrapped in 300 pounds of chain, and was kept under watch. He received visits from members of the gentry and public sentiment was with him, due to his ethos of non-violent thievery. Nevertheless, he too was executed, but Wild did not attend because he was still convalescing from his throat wound.

Soon after he recovered, Wild staged a violent jailbreak to free one of his thieves. This went badly, public sentiment turned against him, and he was sought by the authorities. He was sent to Newgate prison but continued to run his empire from there. He was brought to trial for the violent jailbreak and for stealing jewels from the Knights of the Garter. When it was obvious that the public had turned against him, Wild's former accomplices began giving evidence against him. He was sentenced to death. Unmanned, he broke down and begged for his life, but the court was impassive. In prison, he developed gout, was in constant pain from it, and lapsed into complete insanity. On the day of his execution he tried to commit suicide by drinking laudanum, but threw it all up and went into a coma. He was hanged anyway, still in the coma, at one of the largest public hangings in London. The same public that sang his praises earlier now cheered his death. Tickets were even sold for the best views of the hanging.

His body was buried, in secret, next to his third wife. But later in the century, when autopsies were being conducted on famous criminals, doctors dug up his body and studied it. His skeleton is still on display at the Hunterian Museum.

Wild captured the attention of writers such as Daniel Defoe, who wrote an account of his life, and was the inspiration for Peachum in John Gray's *The Beggar's Opera* (Sheppard is represented by Macheath, who would live on the 20th century as the inspiration for Bobby Darin's "Mack the Knife").

So, for leaving his wife and son, abusing his legal authority, betraying the public trust, cutting off Molly's ear when he was done with her, turning on his former friends and associates, bungling a jailbreak, misreading the public's admiration of Jack Sheppard, begging for his life when he'd ignored similar pleas from his former friend Blake, and for failing in his suicide attempt, I think we can safely say that while Wild might not have been a complete jackass, he comes pretty close, and deserves to be ranked among the Jackasses of History.

Unpleasant Trivia...

• The great composer Mozart was, despite his classy and beautiful music, something of a jackass, at least when it came to scatalogical humor. He once wrote a canon in B Flat major called "Lech mir den arsch fein recht schon sauber"—that translates roughly as "Lick my ass right well and clean." Here's a translation of the lyrics: "Lick my ass nicely, lick it nice and clean, nice and clean, lick my ass. That's a greasy desire, nicely buttered, like the licking of roast meat, my daily activity. Three will lick more than two, come on, just try it, and lick, lick, lick. Everybody lick their ass for themselves." True story.

• The human brain can remain conscious up to 30 seconds after the head has been decapitated. How do we know? In 1905 French and Belgian scientists experimented on convicted murderer Henri Languille. After the guillotine took Henri's head off, the scientists noted that his head looked at and tried to respond to those who called his name for about 30 seconds. Creepy, and just a little cruel...

• Winston Churchill may be the hero of the English people and one of the most admired figures of the 20th century. He showed great courage in the face of near-certain victory by the Nazis. Nevertheless, here is a disturbing quote from him: "I do not admit...that a great wrong has been done to the Red Indians of America, or the black people of Australia...by the fact that a stronger race, a higher grade race... has come in and taken its place." -Churchill to Palestine Royal Commission, 1937. He was also on-the-record as in favor of the use of poison gas on "uncivilized tribes."

A gifted commander, he allowed his personal biases and arrogance to take precedence over military necessity, meanwhile bragging he could be the Dictator of the USA, if he wished.

GEORGE B. MCCLELLAN

Before we talk about why General George B. McClellan, once the general-in-chief of Union forces during the American Civil War, is a Jackass of the First Order, let's talk about his good points. He was handsome. He was charismatic. He was a very good organizer, and academically, understood military tactics and, especially, training.

Unfortunately, he was pompous, vain, prone to bask in unwarranted self-congratulation, ignored orders, was insubordinate to his commanders (especially President Lincoln) identified with the aristocratic south, supported slavery, and, worst of all, seemed overly cautious to the point of cowardice. He blamed all of this failures on others, and history would judge him not only by his contemporary detractors, but by embarrassing revelations found in his own letters and papers after his death.

George McClellan was a blue-blood, born into a wealthy family. He showed early promise, graduating university at 13 and being given a special dispensation to enter West Point early. He graduated second in his class. At West Point his closest friends were Southern aristocrats and he was sympathetic to their lifestyle, believing firmly that slavery was protected by the Constitution.

During the Mexican-American War, he served as a commander of engineers and did well constructing things under fire, although he never saw actual combat as a participant. He wrote a manual on bayonet tactics, but it was only afterward he acknowledged he had simply translated it from the French. After that, he was sent to the West to shore up fortifications and scout out passes through the Cascade Range of the Rocky Mountains. He was utterly insubordinate to his commander, the governor of the Washington Territory, because he considered him a social inferior. Ignoring orders and acting on faulty intelligence, he found a pitiable pass through the mountains, somehow managing to miss three far better ones that were quite close by. These would later be used by the railroad companies. This process took him so long that he was presumed dead, and he was bitter about newspaper articles that reported he'd been killed by Comanches. He refused to surrender his log books when he was relieved of command; it later turned out this was because of embarrassing personal comments he made about his commanding officers.

He soon became a protege of future Confederate president Jefferson Davis, who sent him on a secret mission to the Dominican Republic with an eye toward future annexation. His ties with the south were strong. He believed in the Union, but felt that the Federal government should not interfere with slavery.

When the Civil War broke out, he claimed a great victory at the Battle of Rich Mountain. It wasn't much of one—it was, in truth, somewhat indecisive, although the Confederates did withdraw. Faced with many Union setbacks at the outbreak of the war, the public nevertheless hailed McClellan as a hero, calling him the

"Napoleon of the United States." He seems to have taken this seriously, as his pose in various photographs makes clear. Never mind that during the battle, he threw his own subordinate, commander William Rosecrans, under the proverbial bus by not committing reserve troops to reinforce Rosecrans, which was an essential part of the battle plan, resulting in a Pyrrhic victory.

He became so popular he wrote that if he wished, he could be Dictator of the United States. Because he was a good organizer and had the public on his side, Lincoln put him in charge of the Army of the Potomac, charged with defending Washington DC from the Confederate forces of General Joseph Johnston, who were massed nearby—far too close for comfort.

McClellan boasted that he would crush the rebels in a single campaign, then proceeded to sit around and do pretty much nothing for a few months. He consistently over-estimated the size of the Confederate forces, falling victim to tricks that even the simplest recon missions could have penetrated. For example, Johnston painted tree trunks to look like canon; he marched the same few troops through a gap in McClellan's sight-line over and over and over to give the impression there were more of them than there were (they were just walking in a large circle). McClellan had the largest unit ever assembled in the United States, and one of the largest in the world at the time. Nevertheless, he felt he was not in a position to attack. At no point during his command did McClellan's forces not outnumber his enemy by at least two to one, and often the ratio was far greater.

Meanwhile, he wrote scathing remarks about abolitionists, and issued a proclamation to southerners that he would not free their slaves if he invaded, and would ensure that their property was not damaged (a promise he could not possibly have kept). This was done without the knowledge of his superior, General-in-Chief Scott, or President Lincoln, which miffed them greatly.

McClellan then threatened to either quit the army or stage a military coup unless he was made General-in-Chief. Lincoln reluctantly agreed, hoping that McClellan's skill as a trainer and organizer would come through. But Lincoln and the war committee became increasingly frustrated at McClellan's apparent lack of zeal, as his army sat encamped and made no moves against the Confederates. At the Battle of Ball's Bluff, McClellan managed to lose despite outnumbering his opponents by three to one. When a Congressional committee called him in to explain, McClellan called in sick. His subordinates testified that he did not share any specific overall strategy with them and they were left without orders during the battle.

McClellan blamed Lincoln for his failures, calling him a "baboon" and "gorilla." When Lincoln came to visit McClellan at his home, he kept the president waiting for half an hour, then had a servant tell the president he had gone to bed.

Under intense pressure from Lincoln to do something, McClellan finally shared a plan to divide the Confederate forces called the "Urbanna campaign." This came to nothing, as McClellan took a long time to prepare. Meanwhile, General Johnston somehow managed to move his entire Confederate army without McClellan realizing it, rendering his tardy and over-cautious campaign plans moot.

Lincoln removed McClellan as General-in-Chief, but kept him in charge of the Army of the Potomac and ordered him to focus on taking Richmond, the Confederate capitol. But he conducted this campaign with a significant lack of zeal, it seemed, and soon developed a reputation for never being where the action was. At the Battle of Malvern Hill, for example, McClellan was 10 miles away, in a boat. Newspapers mercilessly lampooned him for sitting in safety while his men died. When General John Pope of the Union moved his army toward Virginia, McClellan was ordered to reinforce him. McClellan didn't, and this resulted in the loss of the Second Battle of Bull Run. Lincoln realized that McClellan was better at engineering and training, and put him in charge of the fortifications of Washington DC, against the advice of his cabinet. Said Lincoln of McClellan, "If he can't fight himself, he excels at getting others to fight."

But when McClellan had his chance to shine, he blew it. General Robert E. Lee invaded Maryland with the Army of Northern Virginia, counting on pro-slavery citizens there to smooth the way. While Lee stampeded into Union territory, he told his subordinates he was counting on McClellan's reputation for being too cautious and academic. McClellan was ordered to chase Lee, but moved his troops at a mere six miles per day. Then he got his golden ticket: spies discovered Lee's battle plans hidden in a rolled-up cigar. McClellan was ecstatic and wrote to Lincoln that if he couldn't crush the Confederates with this knowledge, he would consider himself a failure and go home.

Of course, he didn't crush the Confederates, he didn't consider himself a failure, and he didn't go home. Catching up with Lee at Antietam, he postponed his attack several times due to early-morning fog. This gave Lee plenty of time to prepare. Ultimately, the battle was called a Union victory, but only because Lee withdrew his much smaller force from the field first. The battle was technically a draw, with no tactical advantage for either side. Lee retreated, but McClellan had every opportunity to pursue and destroy the Army of Northern Virginia. Instead, he allowed Lee to maneuver his entire force back across the Potomac into Virginia to regroup and fight another day. In fact, McClellan was many miles away in his tent during the battle, too far away to personally supervise anything. He also, for some reason, chose not to use any cavalry in the battle, leaving a powerful force sitting idle. His subordinates complained that McClellan had shared no overall battle plan with them, making it impossible for them to take initiative or respond to unfolding events during the battle.

Lincoln ordered McClellan's dismissal, replacing him with the famous-whiskered General Burnside. Lincoln also ordered the Emancipation Proclamation at this time. Furious, McClellan ran against Lincoln for president in 1864. But repeated Union victories under his successors doomed his candidacy, and Lincoln won in a landslide. Tellingly, the military voted 3-1 overall in favor of Lincoln, and some 70 percent of the Army of the Potomac voted for Lincoln as well, despite McClellan's personal popularity among the rank-and-file.

McClellan went to Europe after the war, and planned to return and run for President again following Lincoln's assassination. However, he backed out when he learned that Ulysses S. Grant would oppose him. He was appointed to be the Superintendent of Public Works for New York, but the senate blocked the appointment, citing his incompetence. He was elected the governor of New Jersey, where he spent a single term somehow not managing to stir controversy or screw anything up.

He wrote a book defending his conduct in the war, a volume full of bitterness toward his superior officers, blaming all of his failures on Lincoln's refusal to give him enough troops—ridiculous, when we consider he constantly outnumbered his opponents. McClellan died unexpectedly from a heart attack at 58 years old. Neither of his children had children, thus saving future generations from the jackassery in his gene pool.

McClellan went to his grave believing history would vindicate him, but ironically it was his own pen that doomed his reputation. His personal letters to his wife were made public after his death, revealing his tendency for self-aggrandizement and self-congratulations, scathing racist remarks, and total identification with the aristocratic southerners he was supposed to be fighting. History can only conclude that McClellan enjoyed all the trappings of being a general, had a solid understanding of war from an academic point of view, but was reluctant to fight, either from cowardice or because he sympathized too greatly with his enemies.

So, for being pompous and self-important, racist, blaming his inactivity and failures on others, refusing to share battle plans with his subordinates, staying miles away from the front lines of any battle, for publicly snubbing and mocking the commander-in-chief, for terrible political judgment, for prolonging the most terrible conflict in American history through his inaction—congratulating himself all the while as the "savior or the Union" in letters to his wife—General George McClellan is, without a doubt, one of the true Jackasses of History.

Great at racking up debt and bad at paying it off, he turned to homicide to make ends meet. He managed to hide the murder weapon so well he couldn't find it—but roadwardens did.

JOHN THURTELL

John Thurtell (rhymes with "turtle") was known to his friends and family as "Jack." That's appropriate, as few Jackasses of History approach the level of jackassery Thurtell achieved in his short, tragic life. About the only thing he did right was die without (much) drama. He was a confidence man and a murderer. If you're going to be one of those, make sure you're good at it, or, like Thurtell, you'll end up at the end of a rope.

Thurtell was born in the late 18th century into a wealthy family in the English town of Norwich. His father was a prominent merchant and city councilman who also served as mayor. Thurtell shared his father's ambition, but lacked his skill. Rather than apply himself to his studies, he was mad for competitive sports, mainly horse racing and prize-fighting (boxing). After one too many tussles, his father decided a career in the navy would do young Thurtell good, so at age 15, with a freshly purchased commission, he joined Company 99 of the Royal Navy and set out on the HMS Adamant—which promptly sailed to the Firth of Forth in Scotland, and docked for a few years. Other than raising hell in local taverns and insulting the Scots, it appears Thurtell and his crew mates spent their time doing pretty much nothing. When the fleet got a new commander, Thurtell was disciplined and discharged by Rear Admiral William

Otway for some misconduct. We don't know what he did, but they didn't kick you out of the Royal Navy on a whim. Record-keeping slip-ups ensured Thurtell found another berth on the HMS Bellona, despite not technically being in the Navy.

Of course, when Thurtell proudly returned home in 1814, he told his friends and family about his gallant action as he stormed the port of San Sebastian on the north coast of Spain. Naval records prove that his stories of action on the Bellona were baloney. It was docked at the Isle of Wight during the battle, and merely cruised past San Sebastian several days after hostilities had died down. He also told a story of how the Bellona captured a brig of war. It was, in fact, an unarmed merchant schooner that surrendered without a fight.

Thurtell's father arranged for local merchants to extend credit to his son to set up business with his friend Giddens as manufacturers of bombazine, a fancy twilled silk dress fabric that was popular at the time. However, Thurtell soon turned back to his old obsession with prize-fighting. He made friends with a boxer from London who'd moved to Norwich to seek easier pickings. His tales encouraged Thurtell to make regular visits to London, where he frequented disreputable taverns and gambling houses devoted to betting on horse races, prize fights, and other sporting events. At this time, Thurtell impressed his contemporaries, one of whom described him as "a man of integrity."

Thurtell's jackassery was soon exposed, however. While Giddens plugged away managing the bombazine business, Thurtell was often absent from Norwich, and was chronically short of funds. The partners soon became delinquent in payments to their creditors, to the embarrassment of Thurtell's father. When a London mercantile firm purchased several thousand pounds (that is, £, a huge sum at the time) worth of silk, the gallant Thurtell offered to travel to London (alone) to collect the payment. Lo and behold, he returned without the money, saying he'd been ambushed and robbed by footpads. He helpfully displayed some bruises and a small cut on his head as evidence. His creditors, however, were quite vocal about not believing him. His father's influence ensured Thurtell was not charged with a crime, but his reputation in Norwich plummeted, as did that of the over-trusting and innocent Giddens. Their partnership went bankrupt in 1821.

It was a bad year for the Thurtell family—his brother Tom had attempted the simple life of a gentleman farmer, but found it not so simple. Owing £4000 in debt, he soon followed his big brother into bankruptcy (though he owed half of that to his father, so his credit was better than Thurtell's). He blamed his failure on excessive taxation and sub-standard seeds.

The two brothers fled to London, their bankruptcy cases still not discharged by the court in Norwich. The two launched various schemes and enterprises, usually under Tom's name but with Thurtell as the mastermind (if you can call it that) and active agent. Jack came up with a plan to get both he and Tom out of trouble by exploiting the Act of Relief for Insolvent Debtors, recently passed by Parliament. Thurtell believed there was a loophole. Tom was, of course, the Guinea pig. Thurtell lent his brother 17 pounds, and, as arranged, Tom defaulted on the loan. Thurtell then had Tom thrown into King's Bench prison for debt. They banked on this expediting Tom's original bankruptcy case and having it forgiven. This was a staggering mistake, as Thurtell missed some of the finer points of the Act. He

let Tom languish in prison for 14 long months before
finally withdrawing the complaint. Tom appears to have
left London immediately after being released, but this
didn't stop Thurtell from continuing to do business
under his brother's name.

Thurtell took out a lease on a tavern called,
appropriately, The Cock (in Tom's name). He
immediately sold off the contents of the basement
(which did not belong to him). He also purchased a
warehouse in both he and Tom's name. Using proceeds
from the sale of the stuff in the basement, Thurtell made
a down payment to finance hundreds of pounds (£) of
bombazine. He stored it in the warehouse and took out
an insurance policy on it all for some £2000. He spent a
few more pounds making alterations to the warehouse
so that no one could see inside. Then, under cover of
darkness, he transferred the silk to another location
and sold it for cash, making a huge immediate profit
(since he'd mostly paid with credit). Then, surprise!
The warehouse mysteriously burned down—Thurtell's
remodeling job ensured the night watch didn't see the
fire until it was too late.

But the local constable was suspicious. There were
no tell-tale remains of silk in the warehouse, and the
remodeling obviously served no purpose other than to
hide the interior. The county fire office refused to pay
the insurance claim. Thurtell, in Tom's name, sued the
office and won, but the director of the fire office still
refused to pay the claim, and in fact used his contacts to
procure an indictment against Thurtell and the hapless
Tom for conspiracy to defraud the insurance company.
This would eventually come back to bite Tom in the ass.

Most of Thurtell's money slipped through his
fingers in the gambling dens. He fled The Cock and

the mountain of unpaid bills he'd racked up running it and went into hiding under an assumed name at another tavern. During this time, his friend Joseph Hunt wrote that Thurtell "suffered from an observable disintegration of his personality." He spent much time drinking and brooding on his ill-fortune, and writing lists of grievances against all those he'd imagined had wronged him. Chief among them was William Weare, a notorious but non-violent underworld figure who seems to have started as a waiter, then moved to professional gambling. Thurtell had, in his depression, lost £300 to Weare, and it rankled to the point of obsession. He refused to pay, and spread rumors that Weare had only won by cheating. He said because of Weare, he'd become a laughing-stock (not, of course, through his own jackassery).

In October 1823, Thurtell decided on a way to avoid paying Weare the £300 he owed him. Feigning reconciliation and vowing to clear the debt, Thurtell invited Weare for a weekend in the country at the cottage of a friend, Bill Probert. However, Thurtell had enlisted Probert and another crony, Joseph Hunt, to murder Weare (how, we'll never know, but the two were also debt-ridden ne'er-do-wells—think of them as assistant jackasses). The plan was that Thurtell would hire a gig (a gentleman's carriage) and drive to the village of Radlett. Probert and Hunt were to follow along, catch up, and then the three would kill Weare. But the assistants got cold feet, and delayed for hours debating whether they should go through with it.

Eventually they decided to go along, but by the time they caught up with Thurtell, he'd already killed Weare—and made a real mess of it, too. Once dusk fell, Thurtell turned into a dark lane near Probert's cottage, produced a pistol from a matched set, and shot Weare in the face. This failed to kill him. The poor bastard managed to escape from the carriage, but did not get far stumbling into the darkness. Thurtell chased him and caught Weare when he tripped over a root. Thurtell drew a knife and slit Weare's throat from ear to ear, then, for some reason, bashed Weare in the head repeatedly with his pistol, until Weare's brains were dashed all over the ground. Thurtell hid the pistol and the knife in a nearby hedge. Then, when Probert and Hunt arrived, they helped him throw the body into a pond on Probert's property—after searching it and looting it, of course. The trio then went to Probert's cottage, where Thurtell presented Mrs. Probert with a gold chain he'd taken off Weare's corpse.

The next day, Thurtell went to retrieve the murder weapons—but he couldn't find them. Nervous, the men waited for dark, fished Weare's body out of the pond, and dumped it in another pond by the road to the village of Elstree. Meanwhile, a road maintenance crew found the pistol and knife, and saw the brains and blood, and notified authorities. It wasn't long before they showed up looking for Thurtell—whether they were skilled investigators or not is moot. Thurtell, jackass that he was, made it easy for them. All of Weare's friends knew he'd planned to spend the weekend with Thurtell. When he didn't show up at his regular haunts the following Monday, they reported it. The horse Thurtell had hired to pull the gig had rare and distinctive coloration—all gray, with a white face. Several witnesses on the road remembered seeing it, and Thurtell and Weare, riding along on the day of the murder. When the authorities questioned Thurtell, they found the other pistol from the matched set, which was, of course, identical to one of the murder weapons.

At this, Probert and Hunt immediately turned King's Evidence against Thurtell and told everything. All charges were dropped against Probert, but Hunt, who initially lied to investigators about helping to hide the body, was banished to Australia (where, settling in Botany Bay, he married, had two children, and became a pillar of the community). Thurtell proclaimed his innocence throughout his arrest, confinement, and trial. He attempted to delay the trial by calling witnesses who he knew to be absent from London. This tactic didn't work. He was convicted of Weare's murder and hanged in January 1824. Meanwhile, Hunt sold his story to the newspapers, and the lurid details of the crime ensured a major media circus at the execution. Oddly, Thurtell seems to have died well, without any blubbering or begging. On the scaffold, he admitted to the murder, said justice had been done, and then, in a classic jackass move, instead of asking for forgiveness, announced,"I forgive the world!" His body was dissected and studied and today his skeleton is still on display at the Anatomical Museum of Edinburgh University.

Later that year, his brother Tom was convicted in the warehouse insurance fraud scheme, even though his only crime was to let Thurtell write his name on the paperwork. He, too, was hanged.

Thurtell became something of a celebrity after his death as the subject of penny dreadfuls and cautionary tales about the dangers of young gentlemen coming to London and getting involved in the vice of underworld gambling. But it seems clear that Thurtell's jackassery began long before his gambling days, and we must conclude that he is, indeed, one of the true Jackasses of History.

He could have been a Great Man of State, but he bit the Queenly hand that fed him, grossly overestimated his power and influence, and ruined every "second chance" he got.

ROBERT DEVEREUX, EARL OF ESSEX

We return to Elizabethan England for our next Jackass of History. Meet Robert Devereux, 2nd Earl of Essex (we'll follow convention and call him Essex), who can rightly claim the title of Jackass. He was good-looking, articulate, well-educated, artistic, an accomplished poet, and, when he felt like it, a good soldier. By the time he was 30 he'd reached the pinnacle of what secular utopia can offer most men—and then he proceeded to throw it all away.

Essex's mother was Lettice Knollys, widely regarded as one of the most beautiful women in England. In fact, Queen Elizabeth would later have her banished from court out of jealousy. His godfather, Robert Dudley, Earl of Leicester, was the Queen's favorite (and probably the only man she'd ever loved). She couldn't marry him—he was her social inferior, was not well-liked, and was something of a jackass himself. But she kept Dudley close. She was furious when Dudley secretly married Knollys, becoming young Essex's stepfather. The Queen took an interest in Essex—he was related to Mary Boleyn, sister of the Queen's ill-fated mother Ann Boleyn. She placed the titled youngster in the home of her closest, most trusted adviser, William

Cecil, Lord Burghley. There, he met Burghley's son, the
hunchbacked Robert Cecil, and the two became lifelong
enemies.

Essex was an ambitious young man, and did not lack
courage. He saw military action in the Netherlands
under Dudley's command, fighting the Spanish. He
distinguished himself at the Battle of Zutphen, in which
his friend and fellow poet Sir Philip Sidney was killed.
Returning, he was now a man come into his own
estates and left the Cecil household. Arriving at court,
he quickly ingratiated himself with the Queen, who
was now elderly and loved the company of articulate,
handsome young men. She made him Master of Horse
(a ceremonial title once held by Dudley) and gave him
a monopoly on the sale of sweet wines, infuriating the
council and merchants of London.

Eventually Essex managed to weasel his way into
the Privy Council, which galled the Cecils to no end.
Essex quickly gained a reputation for being openly
disrespectful. Not only did he call the Cecil's judgment
into question, he publicly questioned the Queen's
judgement and made rude comments about her. He
also took to mocking Robert Cecil's hunched back
and peculiar way of speaking. Ultimately, he began
to disrespect the Queen to her face. Once, during a
council discussion of the abysmal military situation in
Ireland, the Queen was angered with something he said
and violently boxed him about the ears. In a stunning
display, he half-drew his sword on the Queen before he
was restrained. Everyone expected the Queen to execute
Essex, but she forgave him after a few days of keeping
him confined to his rooms.

Essex then asked the Queen for permission to join Sir
Francis Drake's English Armada, which was intended

to follow-up and exploit the destruction of the Spanish Armada against England. She forbade him to go, but Drake wasn't aware of this and took Essex along anyway. However, Essex became disillusioned (or bored, or resentful of Drake's practice of making gentlemen work alongside his sailors), and he returned home when the fleet failed to take the Spanish-controlled Portuguese port of Lisbon. The Queen was angry, but, predictably, forgave him. He seems to have counted on this over and over throughout his career.

Essex made a good marriage for himself, hooking up with Sir Philip Sidney's young widow, who happened to be the daughter of Elizabeth's feared spymaster Sir Francis Walsingham. Thus protected to some degree, he continued to irritate the Queen's other advisers, particularly the Cecils.

He wasn't a complete incompetent when it came to soldiering, and he was eventually sent to France to defend the temporarily Protestant King Henry IV from his Catholic enemies. Of course, Henry would later convert to Catholicism, quipping "Paris is worth a mass." He also managed to capture the Spanish port of Cadiz, although not in time to stop the Spanish from sinking all their valuables so the English couldn't claim them. He returned with a few high-ranking prisoners, however.

Meanwhile, he continued to alternate between love and disrespect toward the Queen, his behavior causing regular scandals and discomfort for pretty much everyone else. The court marveled at the license Elizabeth allowed Essex. She was known to coddle her favorites, but she did so with Essex more than any other courtier. Some 32 years his senior, she cannot have actually believed there could be love between them, but it seems she did love him in some manner.

Essex begged the Queen to let him lead a fleet against the Spanish, and she allowed it. The so-called Islands Voyage had three prongs—to destroy the Spanish war fleet near the Azores, to occupy the Azores and destroy Spanish settlements there, and to intercept the Spanish treasure fleet on its way back from the Americas. All of this Essex failed to do, blaming his second-in-command, his hated court rival for the Queen's attention, Sir Walter Raleigh. Ignoring the war fleet, he chased the treasure fleet unsuccessfully. Meanwhile the war fleet sailed straight toward England, and was only turned back by storms. The expedition returned in shame, with a public war of words about whose fault it was.

Nevertheless, Essex was popular and charismatic enough that he headed up one of two powerful factions in the elderly Queen's court. The other was led by Robert Cecil, who had by now replaced his father as Elizabeth's chief councilor. Each faction tried to minimize the influence of the other by nominating opponents to take over the role of Lord Lieutenant of Ireland, where the rebel Earl of Tyrone, Hugh O'Neill, was regularly humiliating English forces. Eventually, the chess game ended and Essex was left as the only reasonable choice. Forced by politics, he had to go, leaving Cecil in London to advise the Queen without Essex's influence. Essex was terrified that Cecil was negotiating with King James of Scotland (who, as the son of the doomed Mary, Queen of Scots, had the best claim to follow Elizabeth to the thone). Perhaps because of this, he conducted the war in Ireland without vigor. He led the largest force England had ever sent to Ireland—some 16,000 men plus cavalry and five warships—but didn't use them aside from some inconclusive skirmishes. Meanwhile, he abused his power to confer knighthoods (one even the Queen used sparingly) so much that after the Irish wars, more than half the knights in England owed their status to Essex.

Essex met secretly with O'Neill, using his new stepfather, the Catholic Sir Christopher Blount, as a go-between (Dudley had died by now, but Knollys was still quite marriageable). No one knows what the two discussed, but very soon after, Essex signed a truce with O'Neill that many thought embarrassing to the English cause. He wrote to Elizabeth asking to come home, but she refused. He ignored her order and, leaving Ireland in the care of two subordinates, sailed home. Four days later, he shocked the Queen by barging into her bedchamber in the early morning before she was dressed, and, worse, before she'd put on her wig. Elizabeth ordered him confined to his rooms, but Cecil and the Privy Council were livid when it became apparent that he would, again, go unpunished. Interestingly, well after Elizabeth and Essex were gone from this world, a Spanish ambassador's letters were discovered, in which he wrote that O'Neill told him he'd offered an alliance with Essex, who accepted. It may or may not be true, but the ambassador's correspondence was private, and it has the ring of truth to it.

Five days later, the council called him to stand during a rigorous five-hour interrogation. Within 15 minutes after it was over, they sent the Queen a report saying Essex was guilty of dereliction of duty and that his truce with O'Neill was illegal. The Queen ordered him to be placed under house arrest. Here he wrote scathing letters blaming Cecil and Raleigh for poisoning the Queen's mind against him. Between those two, they did manage to see that Essex was stripped of his sweet wine monopoly, which devastated him financially. During his confinement, it seems he also wrote to King James of Scotland, offering to replace Cecil in securing the succession for James. Nothing came of this.

Eventually, it became clear the cessation of hostilities hadn't been a terrible idea—it at least had given the English a chance to regroup and rethink the Ireland strategy (which some would argue they still haven't figured out). There was even talk that Essex would be sent back to Ireland to redeem himself. But Cecil saw to it that instead, he was hauled before a tribunal of 18 men, who forced Essex to listen, on his knees, to hours and hours of testimony against him. In the end, they found him guilty of malfeasance and sent him to the Tower of London, but Elizabeth commuted this to house arrest. The next summer she released him, but did not restore him to favor. He became deeply depressed, vacillating between begging forgiveness and fits of accusatory rage.

In the winter of 1601, he began the suspicious act of fortifying Essex House, his London manor. He also gathered to his side all of his loyal followers. One morning, completely stymied and overcome with rage against Cecil, he gathered some 300 armed men, including fellow nobles Sir Christopher Blount and Sir Henry Wriothesley (son of one of Henry VIII's chief councilors and the "fair youth" of Shakespeare's sonnets) and marched on Nonsuch Palace, where the Queen was staying. His intention seems to have been to force an audience with the Queen. But Cecil rightly recognized this as treason, and threw up a barricade at Ludgate Hill. Essex's men stormed the barricade, but were beaten back when Blount was injured. They returned to Essex House and holed up, but Crown forces quickly surrounded and besieged the house. Only then did Essex surrender, and even as he was led away, said the Queen would see his side of things if only he could talk to her alone.

That never happened. He was tried and convicted of treason, after making a fool of himself by laying ridiculous counter-charges against Cecil, namely that he was conspiring to place the young princess of Spain on the throne (Cecil was about as Protestant as it was possible to be). Then, oddly, he shocked everyone by accusing his sister, Penelope, Lady Rich (the subject of Sidney's love poems, by the way) of treason. The Queen ignored this charge and never followed it up. Essex was convicted of treason and sentenced to death. Even then, the Queen hemmed and hawed a bit about actually signing the execution order. He probably would have gotten away with it. But, jackass that he was, he ordered one of his soldiers from Ireland, Captain Thomas Lee, to capture the Queen and force her to sign a warrant to free Essex. Lee was apprehended while lurking outside the Queen's chambers.

This seems to have been the last straw for Elizabeth. It is said she wept as she signed the execution order. Essex was beheaded in the Tower of London—the last person ever to be beheaded there. The executioner botched the job, taking several tries to actually sever Essex's head. Blount was also executed, but Cecil convinced the Queen to commute Wriothesley's sentence to life in prison (he'd later be released under King James).

So, for throwing away his natural gifts, biting the hand that lifted him to prominence, conspiring with enemies of the state when his pride was threatened, and for a gross overestimation of his influence and power, Essex rightly deserves to be enshrined in the ranks of Jackasses of History.

He fought bravely at Waterloo and earned a knighthood. He could have retired with honor, but took one final mission for Queen and Country—and managed to lose an entire army.

WILLIAM ELPHINSTONE

Some jackasses are born that way. Others develop jackassery later in life, and Major General William George Keith Elphinstone seems to be one of them. He managed a respectable, even noteworthy, military career until he was nearly 60 years old. Then he was sent to Afghanistan and fell from grace. He is, in fact, the only British general in that nation's history to have lost virtually an entire army. His lack of leadership got his army slaughtered, undermined the reputation of Britain for invincibility, ensured the murder of more than 10,000 civilians, and literally gave his superior, Lord Auckland, a stroke.

In the beginning, though, Elphinstone showed promise. He was born in Scotland in 1782 to one of the directors of the all-powerful British East India Company, which one commentator has described as "like Exxon with guns." His uncle was the great hero Admiral Sir George Elphinstone, who had distinguished himself in the Napoleonic wars. He was, in fact, present when Napoleon surrendered and wrote scathingly of the would-be emperor, calling him "unimpressive" and "ridiculous."

Young Elphinstone, future jackass, was present at Waterloo, leading a regiment of footsoldiers and fighting bravely, earning three knighthoods in England, the Dutch republic, and Russia. It was at this point, perhaps, that Elphinstone should have retired and been remembered as a fine soldier. But...

In 1841 he was sent to Afghanistan and placed in charge of the British garrison at Kabul. Big mistake. Within a few months, nearly everyone who relied on him was dead or sold into slavery. He'd be dead before the end of the year, having humiliated Great Britain and ruined his reputation.

The British, fearing Russian influence in Afghanistan would threaten her possessions in India, had invaded, deposed the ruler Dost Mohammed Khan, and set up a puppet ruler, Shuja Shah, in Kabul. Meanwhile Dost Mohammed had escaped to Bala Hissar, a mountain fortress, and his son Akbar Khan was storming around Afghanistan waging an effective guerilla war against the British and their Indian minions (er, allies).

The British had been paying "subsidies" to various Afghan tribes—payments which essentially amounted to bribes not to attack, and with a few exceptions such as the hot-headed Akbar Khan, it was working. But, concerned about the costs associated with this policy and maintaining a garrison of some 700 British and 3,800 Indian troops (along with as many as 12,500 civilians—wives and children of officers, servants, and so on), the British government decided, at the advice of Sir William Macnaghten, envoy to the Afghani court, to stop the payments. Macnaghten's advisers warned him this was a terrible idea, but he did it anyway. The British also, as a diplomatic overture, did not occupy the nigh-impregnable citadel in Kabul, and instead pitched their camp about one and a half miles away. The situation was far from perfect.

Nevertheless, Kabul was relatively calm, and was the

center of society for the wives and children of the British and Indian officers who were stationed in Afghanistan, even those stationed in other places such as Khord and Jalalabad. Lady Sale, the wife of Major General Sir Robert Sale of the Jalalabad garrison, lived here and was the center of society, importing wine and champagne, throwing regular parties and putting on Shakespeare plays. All the while, this glitz and glitter was surrounded by tens of thousands of relatively irritable Afghanis.

Into this imperfection strode our jackass, Elphinstone. Almost immediately after he arrived, there was a revolt in Kabul (a direct response of the British failure to keep paying bribes to the tribal chieftains). Acting with lightning speed and giving no warning, Akbar Khan stormed the Kabul house of Sir Alexander Barnes and killed him, along with his entire household staff.

The situation died down fairly suddenly, and Elphinstone sent the hapless Macnaghten to negotiate a truce with Akbar Khan. It was, remember, Macnaghten who'd recommended the cessation of subsidies and the overthrow of Khan's father, so he may not have been the best choice. Nevertheless, Macnaghten dutifully showed up to the parlay, even though a group of cavalry Elphinstone promised to send as escort never showed up. Akbar Khan politely invited Macnaghten to take tea with him, then, when they sat to enjoy their beverage, put a pistol in Macnaghten's mouth and pulled the trigger.

Obviously, the British were enraged, their sense of fair sportsmanship quite offended and their utter failure to understand the Afghani mentality embarrassingly exposed. Elphinstone's men were ready to lead a counter-attack on the city while they were still at strength. A strong message must be sent, they advised.

What did Elphinstone do? Nothing. Not so much as a statement of condemnation. Perhaps he was worried for the safety of the civilians, but his own officers sent a formal deputation to beg him to take action. He refused, and gave no reasons for his refusal (at least not on the record). The officers begged him to at least strengthen the defenses of the British supply fort, which was inside the city walls, but he declined to do so, and it fell soon thereafter, leaving the garrison perilously short of vital supplies. They recommended he move the British camp to a more defensible position atop a nearby hill. Elphinstone declined. They recommended instead that he take the citadel in the city, which could be easily defended. For whatever reason, Elphinstone declined.

This stalemate lasted some 20 days, but Elphinstone did not send for reinforcements or make any preparations to strengthen defenses or leave the garrison. Meanwhile, Elphinstone did not send out a force to prevent Khan's men from openly taking a hill that overlooked the British camp, so the British and Indian soldiers enjoyed several days of being bombarded with two of their own captured guns. Finally, Elphinstone ordered a small force to sally forth and take the hill, but they charged into withering fire from long-range jezails (a hand-made musket used by the Afghans). The British troops who led the charge fled back to the camp, leaving some 300 wounded on the field. The Afghanis obligingly climbed down from their hill and slaughtered the wounded to the last man.

At this point, Elphinstone decided maybe it wasn't such a bad idea to send for reinforcements from the British garrison at Kondohar, but he didn't realize that at this time of year, the passes would be hopelessly blocked with snow. Needless to say the reinforcements never arrived. Elphinstone instead sent a second negotiator to speak to Akbar Khan, since it worked out so well the first time. Major Eldred Pottinger made an arrangement with Khan that Elphinstone personally approved, and it contained some regrettable, even humiliating, terms. Elphinstone agreed to turn over all of the gunpowder reserves, leaving only what his soldiers carried on them. He also turned over all the newest muskets and all but six of the garrison's canon. In return, Khan promised safe-conduct for the garrison and its 12,500 dependents to leave for Jalalabad, where Lady Sale's husband was stationed.

Despite what happened the last time he made a deal with Akbar Khan, Elphinstone led a column of 700 British soldiers, some 3,800 Indian soldiers, and the 12,500 family members and hangers-on out of Kabul and into the harsh surrounding terrain. They took their six canon with them but were low on powder and balls. However, due to Akbar's promises of safe-conduct, Elphinstone decided it would be wise to leave all of the sick, wounded, elderly and infirm behind in Kabul. Not only were these left to their fate, but so was the puppet ruler Shujah Shah, who was no doubt alarmed (he was assassinated the next year).

Surprise, surprise: as soon as Elphinstone left Kabul, Akbar set fire to the British camp and killed all those sick, wounded, elderly and infirm who'd been left behind. The retreating soldiers could hear the screams and entreated Elphinstone to turn back, but he pressed on. Elphinsone waited for the Afghani warriors who were supposed to guarantee their safe-conduct, but the warriors never showed up. Still, he waited for food and fuel that Akbar Khan had promised—which, of course, never showed up.

Major Pottinger, seeing how they'd been betrayed, begged Elphinstone to take the mountain fortress of Bala Hissar, which Dost Mohammed had lately quit, while they still had time, manpower and enough powder, there to await reinforcements in the Spring. But Elphinstone decreed there would be no turning back, and pressed on despite little food, fuel, or ammunition, through hostile territory.

On the second day, the slow-moving column suffered sniper attacks from the hills all day long. The civilian followers were so terrified they slowed the army's progress to a mere six miles that day. Several times, forays of Afghani tribesmen raided the lines, capturing all but two of the British canon. Rather than deploy his remaining canon, Elphinstone ordered they be destroyed to prevent them falling into the hands of the enemy.

That afternoon, who showed up but Akbar Khan. He visited Elphinstone and claimed complete ignorance of the attacks, and said the British left too early for him to arrange the supplies and safe-conduct he'd promised. He asked Elphinstone to stop his column and wait while Akbar negotiated with the Ghilzai tribe for safe-passage for the British through the Khord-Kabul pass through the Hindu Kush mountains. Elphinstone agreed, despite the fact that no fully competent man would have trusted Akbar at this point (hell, even Akbar's own father would later poison him). But Elphinstone not only complied, he sent several English hostages with Khan.

Now, as the column approached the pass, military cohesion and discipline began to break down. When they entered the pass, the British were ambushed by the Ghilzai, who were fighting with the very same muskets Elphinstone had turned over to Akbar Khan.

Turns out, Khan wasn't negotiating safe passage, he was delaying Elphinstone so the Ghilzai had time to set up the ambush. But Elphinstone, either very brave or very stupid (or, to be fair, with no other choice), ordered them to continue their march through the pass. By the end of the day 3,000 of his followers were dead—most from the fighting, but some froze to death, and many committed suicide.

The next day, about half his British soldiers deserted and tried to return to Kabul, but they were slaughtered to the last man. At this point, Elphinstone stopped speaking or giving orders. He merely sat on his horse, staring into the distance and ignoring anyone who tried to talk to him. At this point an unlikely leader emerged—Lady Sale, the socialite of Kabul. She took charge of the women, children and servants and marched them to meet with Akbar Khan. She humbly asked for his protection for these non-combatants. He magnanimously agreed, and returned them to Kabul. There, he killed all the Indians. What happened to all but 12 of the British women is, perhaps mercifully, unrecorded. Then Akbar (almost unthinkably) managed to visit Elphinstone and convince him to surrender as a hostage for the safe-conduct of the rest of his men. He agreed, although he had to have realized by now what the fate of his men would be. Elphinstone was returned in chains to Kabul, where he languished in prison and died several months later. Those who remained—who'd been whittled down to 200 soldiers and 2,000 camp followers—were not given safe conduct after all (and, by now, are you surprised?). They made a brave show of it, however, going through some adventures we won't recount here. In the end, it boiled down to 65 soldiers on a hill with 20 muskets and enough powder and balls for two shots each. The Afghans called for them to surrender, saying their lives would be spared. A British officer shouted "not bloody likely!" and they fought to the death.

A few days later, an assistant surgeon under Elphinstone's command rode into Jalalabad on a wounded horse, which collapsed and died. The survivor, William Brydon, was rushed to headquarters, where the staff asked "what happened to the army?" His famous response: "I *am* the army."

The massacre of 16,500 people under British protection shocked the world at the time, and when Lord Auckland, Govenor-General of the region, heard the news, he literally had a stroke and was obliged to return to England.

Later that year, to prove that all of them weren't Knights of the Order of the Jackass, the British sent an "Army of Retribution" to Kabul, and this time they weren't messing around. They leveled the place. In a heroic happy ending for Lady Sale, who was still alive with 11 other women and 21 children, her husband Sir Robert "Fightin' Bob" Sale rode into hostile territory at the head of a cavalry unit and personally rescued her. However, the collective ego of the British Empire suffered a major bitch-slapping thanks to Elphinstone's jackassery. An investigation found that Elphinstone had, while failing to actually lead his troops, put forth just enough effort to prevent any other officer from stepping up to the plate and doing so. The tragedy now serves as a textbook example in military schools all over the world how the weakness and indecisiveness of a single officer can infest an entire army and utterly compromise its morale.

So, for all that he may have once been a good soldier,

I think it's clear that Elphinstone, for managing to lose an entire army when it could have been prevented, can fairly claim a spot in the ranks of Jackasses of History.

Unpleasant Trivia...

• Before he became the first President of the United States, George Washington showed how clever he was. When he was named Commander-in-Chief of the American Army, Washington famously turned down a salary, saying it would not be right for him to profit from such a job. Instead, he suggested that he keep a record of expenses to be reimbursed by the government after the war. That worked out rather well for the Father of Our Country. Instead of getting the $12,000 he would have received as a salary over the time of his service, he turned in, and was fully reimbursed for, exactly $449,261.51. That's some $4.2 million in today's dollars. From September 1775 to March 1776, Washington spent $6,000 on liquor. When he was elected president, he offered not to take a salary in lieu of an an expense account. Congress said "no thanks" and gave him a flat salary of $25,000 a year.

• Before "civilization" came to the Inuit tribes of North America, they managed to thrive in a chilling climate without any modern conveniences. For example, Kleenex. How to combat nasal congestion in Arctic temperatures without tissue paper? Simple. Mothers would literally suck the snot out of their children's noses. Some still do.

• Isaac Newton is rightfully venerated as one of the chief figures in the history of science. Most scientists today would cringe at how Newton actually spent the vast majority of his time. He was a thoroughgoing mystic, obsessed with Biblical chronology and the magical properties of the dimensions of the lost Temple of Solomon. Newton, like some other scientists of his day, was also an Alchemist. He was convinced he was on the cusp of discovering the Philosopher's Stone, an imaginary artifact that could transmute metals into gold, and, Newton believed, prolong his life. Perhaps he was a little embarassed about it: he kept most of his notes of his experiments in code. Even today, some parts of his writing have not been deciphered.

When his experimental model of a parachute didn't work on a dressmaker's dummy, he decided to try it on himself. There's a fine line between brave and stupid—and he crossed it.

FRANZ REICHELT

Meet Franz Reichelt, the Flying Tailor. Well..."flying" might not be the best word. In 1912 he plummeted to his death from the Eiffel Tower in a tragic parachute experiment. This would make him a confident inventor and a brave if foolish fellow, not necessarily a Jackass of History—*if* he'd had any good reason to believe the parachute would work. He didn't, it didn't, and he left a five-inch deep impression of his body at the base of the Eiffel Tower to prove he was here. Jackass or not, that's more than some of us manage to leave behind.

Reichelt was born in Austria in 1879, but moved to Paris when he was about 20 years old. There, he took a room on the third floor of an apartment building and began a career as a dressmaker. He specialized in providing Paris fashions for ladies back home in Vienna, and in catering to mostly German-speaking society ladies in Paris.

But Reichelt had a not-so-secret obsession having to do with clothes. No, he wasn't prancing before his mirror in the ladies' fashions he designed (at least, not as far as we know, and he might have been better off if he had). He was determined to invent a "parachute suit" that would allow a pilot to survive an airplane crash. Aviation was brand-new. It had been less than a decade since the Wright Brothers made their short, if epoch-

making flight in North Carolina. While socializing in the
various coffeehouses and taverns of Paris, Reichelt made
friendly with some early aviators and was fascinated
by their exploits. He was especially inspired by their
stories of the numerous fatal and near-fatal accidents.
These were considered inevitable to some degree, and
all aviators knew the risks. Still, a working, efficient
parachute design was more than welcome. But most
early parachute designs suffered from one glaring
problem—the only ones that worked tended to be fixed
canopies, made with light wood, wire, and canvass, and
had to be fully deployed before they'd work. Obviously,
this wasn't useful to aviators unless they were just
jumping for fun. Also, these tended to work only at very
high altitudes, much higher than a pilot would fly during
the typical military operations of the day. Attempts to
stuff a parachute into a knapsack (basically what we do
now) hadn't been successful, nor had other attempts
to jump from 1,000-2,000 feet, which is what pilots
wanted—that is, something they could open after they
were already on the way down.

In 1910 Reichelt began work on his parachute suit.
It had a few wooden rods and rubber, but it was mostly
a large silk canopy built onto a standard aviator's suit.
It was intended to "fold out" when the pilot opened
his arms, making a cross of his body. His very first
experiments were with dummies—after all, as a
dressmaker he had plenty of dummies laying around
his apartment—and, by all accounts, they seemed to be
somewhat successful. He'd typically drop the dummy
from the fifth floor of his apartment building into the
courtyard. But his prototypes weighed about 150
pounds and used some 65 square feet of material. When
he tried to make it a bit lighter, with a larger "wingspan,"

all of his experiments were failures. One can almost see the battered and broken dress-dummies littering his apartment courtyard.

With his suit still untested by a human, and with a dubious record of success, Reichelt tried to interest the Aero-Club de France into testing his suit. These expert aviators declined. In fact, they told him the canopy was much too weak. They urged him not to waste his time—or, prophetically, risk his life—on further development.

However, Reichelt was unfazed by this rejection, and unmindful of the warning. He continued to drop dummies into the courtyard of his building with marginal, if any, success. The luck he'd had on his earliest tests with the 150-pound design eluded him. Then, in 1911, the Aero-Club announced a prize of 10,000 francs to whoever could invent a safety parachute for aviators, provided the suit weighed no more than 55 pounds. The contest would be open for three years.

Reichelt redoubled his efforts. He reduced the weight to less than 55 pounds at the expense of enlarging the material canopy to about 135 square feet. He attempted multiple experiments with this design. All were failures.

What do you do when your parachute design doesn't work on dummies? Try it yourself? Not unless you're a jackass. Reichelt himself donned his suit and jumped from about 30 feet up. He crashed straight to the ground, but avoided injury by landing in a pile of straw. Oddly—in fact, inexplicably—he tried the same experiment again with no pile of straw from the same height. He broke his leg.

Reichelt felt, with some justification, that his design was sound but that he wasn't attempting the jump from high enough. His friend Gaston Hervieu had tested parachute designs with dummies from the Eiffel Tower.

Reichelt started a campaign to get permission to do
so himself, and after more than a year, permission was
granted (this delay at least gave his broken leg time to
heal).

So, on a cold winter's morning with a stiff breeze
in early 1912, Reichert arrived at the Tower to much
press fanfare and many onlookers. He'd increased the
canopy surface area of his suit to about 330 square feet,
but folded, it was not that much bulkier than normal
aviator's clothing. The design was otherwise essentially
the same as that of all of his failed experiments—the
pilot would make a cross of his body by holding his arms
out, and the material would unfold and create wings and
a 15-foot-high canopy to slow the fall, allowing the pilot
to theoretically land safely, or least non-fatally.

Now, according to press reports, the Prefect of Police
(already under fire for the recent theft of the Mona
Lisa—another jackass for another tale) only gave
Reichelt permission to test dummies from the tower. He
was later obliged to issue a statement saying there was
no way Reichelt would have been granted permission to
make the jump himself.

But that's just what Riechelt did. Keeping it secret
until the last minute, he shocked his friends by
announcing he would do the jump himself. Of course,
one wonders why anyone was surprised, because
Reichelt showed up to the event already wearing the
suit. His friends begged him to use a dummy instead,
and if that worked, try the experiment himself. He was
unmoved. He was so confident of success that he hired
two early film camera operators, one on the ground and
one at the jump point, to record his triumph. His friends
pointed out the high wind, and said that if he must
jump himself, at least wait until the wind died down or

postpone for a nicer day for safety reasons. He refused. They begged him to use a well-waxed safety rope (sort of an early bungie cord that still would have resulted in serious injury). He refused. Finally, fellow parachute experimenter Hervieu, who'd tested dummies from the tower himself, rattled off a long list of technical points that Reichelt had, in Hervieu's opinion, overlooked. According to press reports, Reichelt was unable to answer or rebut any of these points. The frantic Hervieu told Reichelt if he was determined to make the jump, at least make it from higher up than the first deck, which was some 190 feet off the ground. Hervieu said the only way it would work—and he doubted it would—was to make the jump from higher up.

But Reichelt said the suit would prove everyone wrong. He was well aware that only two days before, American daredevil Frederick Law had jumped from the torch-platform of the Statue of Liberty—a jump of some 225 feet—and emerged unscathed (but this was with a fixed, already-open frame canopy). Perhaps this gave him unwarranted confidence. A guard tried to stop him at this point, and there was a long argument. Somehow, Reichelt won, and turned to wave jauntily to the crowd as he climbed to the first deck. There, his friends and a journalist tried to talk him out of making the jump. Again, he shook off their advice.

Reichelt pushed a cafe table next to the railing on the tower's first deck. He put a stool on top of the table, then climbed atop the stool. He placed one foot on the railing, and then stopped and did nothing for about 40 seconds. What was going through his mind in those 40 seconds? We'll never know.

What we do know is that, calmly smiling, Reichelt stepped off the rail, launched himself into the air—and then fell like a rock. The parachute suit half-opened, then wrapped around him, and he crashed into the frozen earth, leaving a five-inch deep impression of his body. His right leg and arm were crushed, his skull and spine were broken, he was bleeding from the mouth, nose and ears, and in a lurid detail the Paris papers couldn't resist including, his eyes were wide open and dilated as if terrified. It was obvious to everyone that he was dead on impact, but he was taken to a hospital anyway.

If you're afflicted with morbid curiosity, simply search the internet for "Flying Tailor" or "Franz Reichelt" and you can see the entire fall in all its gruesome glory. One thing I noticed: it seems to me that maybe, that suit was just starting to open right before Reichelt hit the ground. Maybe, if he'd followed Hervieu's advice to jump from higher up the tower, it would have worked. Again, we'll never know.

Later that year, a Russian aviator named Kotelnikov successfuly tested the world's first "knapsack" parachute, and this is the type of parachute that almost all modern designs derive from. However, it's worth noting that Reichelt's efforts might not have been entirely in vain. In the 1990s, the first working "wingsuits" were produced, and these owe a little bit to Reichelt's early designs.

Reichert also inspired generations of future jackasses. To this day, the Eiffel Tower is a popular spot for illegal base-jumping, and security at the tower is extremely tight.

If any of Reichert's prior tests had shown even a shred of success, he might not deserve to be vilified for one tragic moment of jackassery at the very end of his life. But he ignored the experts, he was cursed with unjustifiable overconfidence, and was obviously more worried about his reputation than his life. In not wanting to look like a jackass by turning around and climbing back down the tower, he showed that he shared what is still a very common failing of macho men everywhere—the attitude that safety is for wimps. So for that alone, and for his spectacular failure to listen to reason, Franz Reichelt is a true Jackass of History.

Unpleasant Trivia...

• Libertarian hero Thomas Jefferson, the third President of the United States, was a lot of things, good and bad. Hypocrite was one of them. He publicly advised that white people should not have children with black people. His own words: "The amalgamation of whites with blacks produces a degredation to which no lover of this country, no lover of excellence in the human character, can innocently consent." Meanwhile, of course, he was having sex—and children—with his slave, Sally Hemmings (herself the illegitimate half-sister of his wife). Jefferson rigorously denied these rumors throughout his life, but it was an open secret. Centuries later, DNA proved it. Double standard!

• Napoleon Bonaparte didn't much care for women, at least outside of romantic purposes. A direct quote: "Nature intended women to be our slaves. They belong to us, just as a tree that bears fruit belongs to its gardener. Women are nothing but machines for producing children." Of course, he was also sexually aroused by female body odor. A surviving letter to his wife, Josephine, warns her that he'll be home soon—so stop washing.

• Gandhi—yeah, that Gandhi—may have been famously celibate, but that didn't stop him from sleeping with young girls. The great man of peace would regularly sleep naked with naked girls in order to "perfect" his celibate state. These included the 16-year-old wife of his nephew and his 19-year-old grandniece. Of course, when it came to talking to their fathers, he didn't give them the "it perfects my celibate state" line. He told their dads he was merely helping them to correct their sleeping postures. One wonders if the ladies practiced passive resistance.

Fearful, indecisive and easily cowed by his mother and powerful nobles, he diminished the power of the crown and paved the way for the Vikings to take the throne of England.

KING ÆTHELRED THE UNREADY

Edgar, King of the English, and his wife, Queen Ælfthryth, must have been proud on a forgotten day in the year 968, when they took their baby boy Æthelred to be baptized...at first. Perhaps when the royal baby took a nice big poop in the baptismal font, they may have had a premonition of his future jackassery. There are bigger Jackasses of History—there are, after all, degrees of jackassery—but Æthelred is certainly one.

To be fair, it's almost certain that "pooping in the font" story is a fabrication. But it's the type of story that, in retrospect, English chroniclers found all too easy to believe. Despite his personal shortcomings as a king, he was handed a heap of problems by his predecessors. Also, in fairness, Æthelred's nickname that has come down to us—"The Unready"—is better translated as "The Ill-Advised." In early English his nickname was Æthelred Unrede, which, if you were living in 11th century England, would have been an obvious pun meaning "Good Advice, Bad (or no) Advice." But, to quote Obiwan Kenobi, "Who's the more foolish? The fool, or the fool who follows him?" Æthelred's chief claim to the ranks of the Jackasses of History is that he was indecisive, weak, and very much ready to take bad advice. He was also a terrible judge of character, trusted no one, was dominated by his ambitious and over-protective mother, was unfaithful in his promises, suffered from tragic procrastination and hesitated to make important decisions. When he did finally make up his mind and take bold, decisive actions, they were usually the wrong ones.

At King Edgar's death, the English lands had only been united under one king for about 40 years. A huge swath of England had been taken over by Danes—Vikings, for lack of a better word—who'd enjoyed rampaging about the island for the previous few centuries. Since 878, when a particularly malignant wave of Danish invaders was defeated by King Alfred the Great, the Danes were (more-or-less) pacified and settled in a region in the east of England called the Danelaw.

This is one of the problems Æthelred inherited. England had an unstable frontier, there were vicious rivalries between powerful noble factions, and an unruly Danish population of questionable allegiance. The times called for a great man. What the times got was Æthelred.

But first they got his brother, Edward. Both he and Æthelred were boys when King Edgar died. They were of very different character and had different mothers. Edward's legitimacy was in question, and there may be some truth to this because Edgar did not officially make him his heir. But this could have been instigated by Æthelred's mother, the strong-willed Aelfhryth, who had ambitions for her son (in a Freudian move, Æthelred would later marry Emma of Normandy, who shared many of his mom's personality traits).

Teenage Edward was a pious sort, and, despite his occasional fits of rage, he was a great friend to the Benedictine monks, granting them lands and honors that made some nobles feel their prerogatives had been trampled on. The English were divided between supporting Edward or Æthelred, but this didn't stop what passed for normal family relations, such as holiday visits. When the young King Edward went to visit his stepmother and little brother at what would later be Corfe Castle, he was murdered by Æthelred's attendants. Civil war nearly broke out over this, and Edward the Martyr, as he became known, would later become a Roman Catholic saint. Of course, one of the first things the nobles did under the reign of Æthelred—who was a mere 13 years old when he took the throne—was to grab back all the lands granted to the monks. It's possible that Æthelred's reputation of jackassery was intensified by those same monks, who, conveniently for those they admired, tended to write the historical chronicles of the day.

The weak young king, easily dominated by his mother and influential nobles, took power under a cloud of suspicion and the disapproval of a hostile church. King Edgar had, during his reign, tightened the screws on the Danelaw and made it subservient to him. But in 980 the Vikings—mostly Danes—began carrying out more attacks, rampaging along the coasts and doing what Vikings do best: rape, murder and pillage (usually in that order). With young Æthelred seemingly inactive, a powerful nobleman, Byhrtnoth, led a force against the Danes and was soundly thrashed at the Battle of Maldon. This was embarrassing, and, what's worse, was merely the first in a long series of humiliating and costly defeats at Viking hands.

Two of the worst offenders were Olaf Tryggvason of Norway, who stormed around the coasts of Kent and East Anglia at will, extorting tribute from locals, and

Sweyn Forkbeard, King of Denmark, who returned with his buddy Olaf in 994 and plundered southern England. They even tried to besiege London, and while this was ultimately unsuccessful, it was a blow to the young king's pride and devastating for London's economy.

Æthelred was faced with a problem: how to get rid of these rampaging, Godless heathens? Here's the jackass solution: he ordered the massacre of all Danish men in England on St. Brice's Day in 1006. Only about a third of English lands complied, because the Danes were too popular everywhere else. But in a case of incredibly poor oversight, Æthelred's agents murdered Gunhilde, the sister of Sweyn Forkbeard of Denmark, who swore to come back and get revenge. And he did, bringing his pal Olaf with him.

Probably on the advice of his noble counselors, Æthelred decided to pay the invaders a handsome bribe to go away. Some 20,000 pounds of silver changed hands. This wasn't a terrible idea on the face of it—after all, even the famous King Alfred the Great had bribed Vikings to go away. But Alfred used the breathing room to reinforce his defenses and train his men to counter Viking tactics. Guess what Æthelred did? Nothing. He reorganized no defensive strategy, reinforced no fortifications.

Understandably, perhaps, the Vikings took this as an open invitation to come back again, do a little more raping, murdering, and pillaging, and hope for a nice big payoff. Predictably to everyone but Æthelred and his advisers, this rapidly became a slippery slope—an uphill slope, that is, of a giant pile of silver.

As the inevitable waves of Norse and Danes stomped around England more-or-less at will (with the occasional setback, it's true), Æthelred upped the ante and in the year 1007 offered 30,000 pounds of silver for them to go away. They did. At this point, someone decided having a navy wouldn't be a terrible idea. Æthelred ordered one built, but when one of its admirals went pirate, he didn't trust the commanders of the fleet and wouldn't use it. The worst blow came five years later under Thorkell the Tall of Denmark, who raped and murdered and pillaged some more, and Æthelred offered him 48,000 pounds of silver to politely cease and desist. This last bribe came a bit too late for some of Æthelred's subjects, including the Archbishop of Canterbury, who was hacked to death by Vikings after they raided Canterbury, looted the cathedral, and "befouled the holy water." So much for Æthelred's strategy of bribery.

This lure of easy money and apparent weakness encouraged Sweyn Forkbeard to come back and begin a full-fledged, once-and-for-all conquest of England. In summer 1013, he invaded, and was so successful so quickly that by fall, the lands of the Danelaw had accepted him as their king, and by the end of the year, almost all of England, heartily sick of perennial slaughter, recognized Sweyn as their king. Æthelred, by now in his mid-20s, was forced to flee to Normandy (part of northern France), where he and his loving momma hid out for less than a year. Æthelred didn't waste time while he was on his forced vacation. His first wife having died, he married Emma, daughter of Roger of Normandy, a wedding that would have very serious implications for England's future. It formally opened diplomatic relations between England and Normandy, but it also started a fateful bloodline and set the stage for the Norman conquest of England several decades later.

Then, with misfortune following fortune, Sweyn died.

The nobles of England were split in loyalty between Sweyn's son Cnut (sometimes spelled Canute) and Æthelred, who was, if nothing else, English. A powerful faction spirited him and his family back into the country and put him on the throne, but not without some significant strings attached. Æthelred was required to swear an oath of loyalty to his nobles, to institute reforms of pretty much everything his nobles didn't care for, and to forgive anything that was said or done against him during his previous reign. All of that was just fine with Æthelred. This is an important historical milestone, because it pre-figures the Magna Carta signed by King John (another jackass) and shows a tradition of strong oversight of monarchy that was always a factor in English history and would ultimately influence the founding of the United States.

At any rate, the very fact that Æthelred was forced to swear such an oath is strong evidence that his nobles didn't trust or respect him, and this is probably why about half of them declared for Cnut. At this point, it was more important for England to have a strong king, they reasoned, than an English one.

But Æthelred and his supporters went to war on Cnut and his allies, who were mostly based in the minor Kingdom of Lindsey. Cnut hadn't quite finished preparing for war when he heard Æthelred's forces were on their way, and he wisely chose to temporarily remove himself from England without a fight. This was, of course, very bad luck for his Lindseyan supporters, whose lands were laid waste by Æthelred in revenge.

However, when he got home, he found his own son, the violent and skillful Edmund Ironside, had revolted against him and established a power base in the Danelaw. So many people were disillusioned with both Æthelred and Cnut that they were ready to support Edmund—or anyone—against either or both of them. Relations between Edmund and Æthelred had always been rocky. Edmund hated his stepmother Emma, and felt threatened by her ambitions for her sons (indeed, her son Edward the Confessor would later become king). Edmund was a bit of a jackass himself, or maybe just more of a jerk. He used Æthelred's reprisals against the Danes to confiscate property, enrich his own estates, and murder his personal enemies. He killed a noble who'd supported Sweyn, one Sigeferth, then married Sigeferth's unwilling wife, Ealdgyth, a move that alienated many (and which was directly counter to his father's wishes).

Within less than a year, Cnut came back to England, stampeded across it, and conquered most of it, which led to a hasty reconciliation between Æthelred and Edmund. But Æthelred suddenly died in the spring of 1016, leaving the way clear for Edmund. Unfortunately, most of the nobles in England liked Cnut a bit better, but Edmund continued the war until he was defeated at the Battle of Ashington. Cnut respected him as a warrior and agreed to split England with him, but Cnut became sole king after Edmund was assassinated several months later (a persistent legend says he was killed with a crossbow while sitting on the privy, Tywin Lannister-style).

Unfortunately, history does not record how Æthelred died, but he probably wasn't ready for it. He was buried with honor in London but his grave and monument were lost during the Great Fire of 1666. It is, perhaps, a fitting end to one of England's weakest kings. But as far as English kings go, Æthelred would certainly not be the last one who was a Jackass of History.

In desperate, hopeless love with Mary Queen of Scots, he was romantic and dramatic to a fault. Jackass that he was, he misconstrued flirtation for true love, and was hanged for it.

PIERRE DE BOCOSEL DE CHASTELARD

Meet Pierre de Bocosel de Chastelard. He was a poet. He was in hopeless, pathetic love with Mary, Queen of Scots, and he died for it. Tragic, yes. Preventable, definitely. And while his intentions were not ignoble and there is good evidence to suggest Mary encouraged him, his unrealistic ambitions and inappropriate behavior surely earn him a place among the Jackasses of History.

Like many jackasses, jackassery was absent from his family tree. Someone, after all, always has to be the first. de Chastelard was born in the southeast of France to a very important family. He was the grandson of the famous Chavelier de Bayard, who had a long French nickname meaning "the knight without fear and beyond reproach." As the third son in his family, de Chastelard could not expect to inherit titles and property. Such sons had three career options available (four if you count sucking up to and living off older siblings, which many did). His options were the Church or the Military—to both of which de Chastelard was totally unsuited—or a career at court. Since his contemporaries thought de Chastelard to be extremely good-looking, not to mention incredibly charming and charismatic, this was his best choice, and he went to serve as a page, first in the household of Constable Montmorency, then in that of Marshall Danville. It was in Danville's service that de Chastelard joined the circles of nobles who made it their business to hang around the court of King Henry II of France, generally kissing ass and hoping for some form of notice or reward.

This turned out to be de Chastelard's undoing, for it was here he met the teenage Mary, Queen of Scots, who was married to the Dauphin (what the French called the heir to the king), Francis. Although Francis was a year younger than Mary, was sickly, relatively unattractive, and small, he'd scored a trophy wife soon after he was born, as King James IV of Scotland and King Henry II of France decided to betroth their youngsters, the better to eventually screw over their mutual enemy, England. After James died (more-or-less of humiliation) after being soundly thrashed by notorious ass-kicker King Henry VIII (who'd hoped in vain to marry his son Edward to Mary), Mary's French mother, Mary of Guise, sent the little girl (who was five years old) to France to be brought up in Paris. Here, she quickly became very popular, because she was extremely beautiful, lively and vivacious, and, in my opinion, was one of those women who, on purpose or by accident, gave every man she ever met the idea that *just maybe* she was in love with him. In fact, pretty much everyone in France loved her except for her mother-in-law, Catherine de Medici, who was (literally) a royal bitch.

And, of course, young de Chastelard loved her, too. He was already writing poetry for her, taking advantage of his reputation of descent from a chivalric family by writing "courtly love" poems, in which the hopeless poet expresses his pure, eternal love for a woman he's well aware he can never be with. It was appropriate at that time to write such poems to royalty or other men's wives, as it was implied in the poetry that the base poet would never dare besmirch the subject's sanctified virginity or marital status by going to far as to actually try to get her into bed. This type of poetry was often publicly appreciated by the subjects. Again—nothing weird about it.

However, Henry II of France died a bit early from jousting injuries, and 15-year-old Francis became king. Mary and Francis appear to have legitimately gotten along well. After all, they'd been raised together since she was five and he was four. Of course, neither of them ruled France—this duty was gladly seized by Francis' and Mary's uncles, the Guise Brothers (the Duke of Guise and the Cardinal of Lorraine). The young royal couple was happy—but not for long. The sickly Francis soon fell victim to an inner ear infection that got out of control, and died of a brain abscess soon after.

After this, de Chastelard's love poems to Mary increased in frequency and intensity. Catherine de Medici became regent for Francis' 10-year-old brother, the new King Charles IX of France, and, never having taken to Mary, sent her back to Scotland.

What does this have to do with de Chastelard? He was devastated, and with some hoop-jumping, managed to get himself assigned to the party that escorted Mary to Scotland. Sent back to Paris, he petitioned again and again to be allowed to go to Scotland and join Mary's court, and, managing to secure letters of recommendation from other poets (who probably wanted him out of the way) and from his important relatives, he arrived in Scotland and joined Mary's court. This article can't get into the complicated, turbulent situation Mary found herself in when she returned to

Scotland. It was a mess made by dozens of jackasses working in unintended concert, and Mary, herself a bit of a jackass, made everything worse with some very bad decisions we'll save for her own article. One of those bad decisions was to allow young de Chastelard way too much license, and permitting him to be over-familiar with her. Some of this—leaning her head on his shoulder or kissing his cheek—wouldn't have raised eyebrows in the permissive, decadent, and intrigue-ridden French court. In Scotland, full of dour, scowling, perennially pissed-off Protestants like John Knox, this was scandalous behavior to say the least. No matter how innocent Mary's attention to de Chastelard, it looked bad, and in politics, that's often all that counts.

Mary was looking for a Catholic husband from among the royalty of Europe, and, after rejecting such possibilities as the Archduke of Austria (because her uncles the Guise Brothers had negotiated without telling her about it first), she set her sights on Don Carlos, the heir to King Phillip II of Spain (yet another jackass, who once tried to force a shoemaker to eat a pair of boots Carlos found sub-standard). Carlos was mentally unstable to say the least, and Phillip wisely kept a pretty short leash on him, so this came to nothing. Perhaps Mary was just lonely, and this is why she encouraged de Chastelard's attentions.

de Chastelard wrote Mary countless love poems, and she responded to many in kind. Her apologetic biographers would have you believe she was merely being polite, but I wonder. Most likely, Mary was frightened, homesick for France, confused about the political situation, and just wanted a friend from the old days. Clearly, she was flattered by de Chastelard's attention, causing the Protestant reformer and firebrand

John Knox to complain that he could never get in to have a meeting with her because she was always busy hanging around with de Chastelard.

Mary showered de Chastelard with gifts, including one of the finest horses in the realm and expensive clothing, and always made it a point to dance with him on New Year's Eve and other celebrations. It was at this point in history that de Chastelard's latent jackassery began to emerge in earnest.

The poet decided it would be an incredibly great idea if he stealthily crept into Mary's private chamber in Holyrood Palace and hid under the bed. He planned to leap out and surprise her once she was alone, and declare his love for her (what he thought would happen after that is anyone's guess). Despite his familiarity with the Queen, he failed to realize her agents did nightly security sweeps of her bedroom, and they found him hiding there.

Rather than being charmed, Mary was furious—maybe more about how it made her look than anything—and she banished de Chastelard from Scotland. However, like many who swear undying love and loyalty, de Chastelard tended to do anything Mary said except one—go away.

Instead, proving to an almost stunning degree how well he deserves his Jackass of History membership, de Chastelard refused to leave, skulked around in hiding for two or three days, and then chose to burst into Mary's private chambers, unannounced, just after she had gotten undressed. Bad idea.

Mary was surprised and angry—after all, de Chastelard was supposed to be back in France—and there probably aren't many ladies then or now, queen or not, who'd appreciate being seen naked by an uninvited guest. She screamed, which alerted her half-brother Morray, who came storming into the room (presumably Mary covered herself with a sheet or something, but who knows?). Morray's men grabbed de Chastelard and detained him. Mary shouted that Morray should stick his dagger in the villain. Morray, however, in the style of the old-school Scottish lord he was, refused to stab someone who was immobilized. Instead, they dragged the hapless de Chastelard down to the dungeons, with him crying his love for Mary and begging her forgiveness the whole way.

His crime was bad enough to warrant some pretty serious punishment. After all, he'd refused an order to leave Scotland, purposely barged into the queen's room when he knew she'd be disrobing, and, what's worse, had a blade on him. That blade was all anyone needed—more than they needed—to establish a charge of treason. He was so charged, and transferred to the dungeons and St. Andrews. Here, he composed numerous well-written and pathetic pleas to Mary to show him mercy, but by this time she was officially ignoring him. After a week in prison he was marched to the scaffold in winter 1563.

Always one for drama, de Chastelard made sure his departure was remembered. He recited a poem about death on his way to the scaffold (he didn't write it). After his head went into the noose and before the trap door dropped, a tearful de Chastelard looked in the direction where he thought Mary might be watching (she wasn't) and cried aloud for all to hear: "Adieu, most lovely and cruel of princesses!" Even this final display of dramatics was seized upon by Mary's Protestant enemies as evidence that the Queen had behaved inappropriately.

As he went to his eternal reward (whatever it was), de

Chastelard could, perhaps, console himself knowing that he would not be the final jackass associated with the hot-but-dumb queen. Both of her subsequent relationships, with Lord Darnley and Lord Bothwell, were completely inappropriate, politically disastrous, and, to be sure, both Darnley and Bothwell were first-class jackasses, too.

But history will always remember de Chastelard, first jackass lover of a jackass queen who was attracted to jackasses. Unrequited love doesn't make you a jackass, but to even think for one minute he could have ended up with Mary, for allowing that love to make him commit stupid, dangerous, and possibly threatening acts, certainly makes de Chastelard one.

A final interesting tidbit—there is at least some evidence to suggest that de Chastelard was a secret agent, working for the English Queen Elizabeth's feared spymaster Walsingham. The theory goes that de Chastelard did everything he did on purpose to destroy Mary's reputation to prevent her marrying a Catholic monarch from Europe. If this is true, de Chastelard certainly went to the gallows with secrecy and grace, so I doubt it. But you never know.

Certainly, Mary Queen of Scots didn't need de Chastelard to ruin her reputation. She managed that just fine on her own.

Unpleasant Trivia...

• In 1858 in the Italian city of Bologna, kidnappers entered a Jewish couple's home and took their son, Edgardo. He'd been secretly baptized by a non-Jewish servant, who feared he'd die and go to hell while sick. Pope Pius IX ignored international pressure to give the boy back, and raised him in the Vatican to become a priest. When the kid grew up, he campaigned for Pius's canonization. Too bad!

It's OK to be bisexual. It's OK to wed a handsome chariot driver. It's OK to dress like a girl. But if you're a Roman Emperor also working as a tranvestite prostitute, you're probably a jackass.

ELAGABALUS, EMPEROR OF ROME

When it comes to Roman emperors, the field is so full of potential jackasses, it's tough to narrow it down. Doubtless we'll get to many of them in time. For now, let's skip over the obvious choices (Caligula, Commodus, Nero) and settle on Elagabalus.

Before we get started, let's get this out of the way— Elagabalus was bisexual, he was a transvestite, and was probably what we would today call transgendered. Lest anyone think these are the reasons for his jackassery, let me say clearly: they're not. That being said, when a Roman emperor thinks it's a good idea to make up his face and hair like a girl and prance around naked in front of the Roman Senate, he's a jackass. Such behavior can't be judged by the standards of our own time, when we pretty much let people be whatever they say they are. Had Elagabalus been a bit older, he might have known better. Even this decadence (at least, that's how the Romans saw it) might have been tolerated, had Elagabalus not engaged in a bunch of other weird and offensive behaviors. It wasn't Elagabalus' sexuality that made him a jackass, but his inability to restrain it for political purposes, combined with religious zealotry...a strange combination.

We can't really blame poor Elagabalus too much. He was, at first, the tool of his mother and grandmother, who had convinced him by the time he was 14 that the sun almost literally shone out of his butt. At that young age he was already the high priest of a cult of a sun god (Elagabalus, a Latinized version of Ilah Gabal, a Middle Eastern name). The hubris of taking the god's name might be evidence of jackassery, but he was never called this in his lifetime. He was born Sextus Varius Avitus Bassianus. He was Syrian by blood and raised in Syria, mostly by his grandmother, Julia Maesa, who would have a huge influence on his life for good and ill, as we'll see.

The family was an important one—Julia Maesa was the aunt of the emperor Caracalla (himself an unpleasant fellow and jackass, which seems to have run in the family). When Caracalla was assassinated and replaced with the leader of his personal bodyguard, Macrinas, Julia Maesa convinced the nearby Third Legion to declare her grandson (Caracalla's cousin) emperor instead. She went so far as to promote publicly the idea that he was Caracalla's illegitimate child (the fact that this would make him a child of incest appears to have disturbed no one) in order to bolster his claim. Contemporaries certainly thought young Elagabalus looked a lot like Caracalla—more closely than cousins should—so who knows?

Macrinus sent an army to Syria to deal with this threat, but, for some reason, the rank-and-file men switched sides at the last minute and killed their officers, sending the head of their leader back to Macrinus in a box. Macrinus had the Senate declare war on Elagabalus (and Julia Maesa by name, showing how powerful she was known to be). Macrinus told the Senate he believed

Elagabalus was insane. Macrinus went to war against Elagabalus but, at Antioch, his Second Legion deserted him and he was defeated. Macrinus fled but was eventually captured and executed (they went ahead and killed his son, too, for good measure).

Elagabalus took this victory to mean he pretty much already was the Emperor, and declared himself as such, flouting tradition by taking all the requisite imperial titles before the Senate ever confirmed them. Nevertheless, the Senate did accept him as Emperor, primarily because of his support among the military.

This military support did not last long. When it came to tolerance of homosexuality, the Romans could not have been more different than, say, the Greeks. Even in the decadent age of the Empire, with the stern, conservative values of the old Roman Republic routinely flouted, gay men kept their passions to themselves, for the most part. Occasionally very powerful men would be more open about it. But it was probably a little less tolerated in ancient Rome than it was in, say, the United States in mid-20th century. The general consensus seems to be the same thing you hear a lot of folks saying now: do what you want but keep it behind closed doors.

Of course, today even the most staunch advocates for the rights of the queer community might feel just a wee bit uncomfortable if the President of the United States dressed like a woman and stood naked in the door of the White House soliciting pay for sex. But that's exactly what Elagabalus did.

Hard to blame him, really—he was a spoiled child, taught since birth that he was essentially God, so we're talking about a megalomaniacal, overly hormonal teenager in charge of the most powerful empire in the world. Not a recipe for success.

Elagabalus almost immediately alienated the military with his sexuality. He wasn't just "open," he did what some might call "flaunting" it, which, again, he had a right to do as a Human Being, but it was at best bad policy for a Roman Emperor. Not only that, he was Syrian, and while this was part of the Empire, the Romans always saw Middle Easterners as despotic, decadent, and overly mystical. Elagabalus did nothing to disabuse anyone of this notion. He took the name Marcus Aurelius Antoninus Augustus in order to connect himself to some of the more popular previous emperors, which was good. He then made the religion of which he was already the high priest—the cult of Elagabalus—the official religion of the state, and officially "demoted" Jupiter. He routinely paraded a rock said to be a meteorite fallen from the sun around Rome, drawn by white horses, and forced everyone to worship it. He was certainly a single-minded religious zealot, which doesn't square with his other behavior, but then again, everyone did think he was insane. Julia Maesa had a portrait of him hung over the statues and portraits of other gods, so no one (to the Roman mind) could worship one without also worshiping Elagabalus. None of this pleased the military, and revolts had broken out and been squashed before the boy ever reached Rome itself. In fact, the Third Legion—the very legion that propelled him to power in the first place—rebelled and had to be put down and disbanded.

Once secure in Rome, he forgave the Senate for declaring against him (except for a few of the ones who annoyed his grandmother the most). Elagabalus then set the tone for his reign by forcing the Senate to participate in religious rites in which he made himself up like a girl and danced nude for hours. He also started up an open sexual relationship with a popular charioteer, Hierocles. He had Hierocles declared "Ceasar, the Husband of the Empress." He awarded riches and titles to several other male lovers, as well, and publicly married a male athlete. But he liked girls, too—he had five wives, switched back and forth between them quite often, and even forcibly abducted, raped, and married (in that order) a Vestal Virgin. These virginal priestesses were so sacrosanct that if a man seduced one he was to be executed, and she was to be buried alive. Needless to say, no one enforced this law on Elagabalus. That being said, Elagabalus would have been happy to do without his penis, as he publicly offered a substantial sum for any physician who could give him female genetalia.

Egabalus at least believed in equality for women— well, his mother and grandmother, anyway, both of whom were made Senators. But, to emperor-making Julia Maesa's horror, her little grandson proved almost impossible to control. He had a will of his own, and once Julia Maesa and his mother (also named Julia) tried to moderate or curb his behavior, they learned he would damn well do as he pleased.

And apparently what pleased him was to paint his face, pleat his hair, and otherwise doll himself up like a girl, then stand naked in the doorway of the palace (this is how prostitutes advertised). He had agents comb the streets for men who "pleased him with their foulness," according to one contemporary historian, so apparently he liked to go slumming. He accepted pay from these men for his sexual favors, then publicly boasted about how much money he made whoring himself out.

This was too much for grandma (Julia Maesa), who thought her daughter Julia, Elagabalus' mother, was part of the problem for encouraging him too much,

especially in his unpopular religious practices. And so
the elder Julia set a plot in motion, turning to her other
daughter (also named Julia!), and her other grandson,
Severus Alexander. She somehow persuaded Elagabalus
to make Alexander his heir and co-consul, but
Elagabalus began to worry that his personal bodyguard
would vastly prefer it if he would die and make way for
Alexander.

Surprise, surprise, several assassination attempts
against Alexander followed, but the wily young
imperial cousin managed to avoid them all. Failing in
this, Elagabalus stripped his cousin of all lands, titles,
and privileges, and then circulated a rumor that he
was near-dead, to see how the military would react.
They rioted and demanded that both Elagabalus and
Alexander appear before them. Elagabalus agreed, and
brought his own mother Julia along for the ride. As
the trio approached, the soldiers all began cheering for
Alexander and pointedly ignoring Elagabalus, meeting
him with stony, sullen silence. In a rage, Elagabalus
declared them all guilty of treason and ordered that they
be executed.

Instead, his own bodyguards rose up against him. He
and his mother ran, and both of them squeezed into a
chest to hide. They were discovered a short time later,
though, and both were beheaded, stripped naked, and
had their corpses paraded around Rome before the
people threw Elagabalus' mutilated body in the Tiber
river. His loving grandma, who more than probably
ordered the whole affair, managed to rule behind the
throne after Alexander was declared Emperor—for a
while. He, too, would be assassinated.

So let the record reflect that Elagabalus isn't a Jackass
of History because of his sexual preferences. Again,

plenty of emperors enjoyed their boy toys on the side. But when the Roman Emperor, dressed as a girl, combed the gutters for the grossest possible low-lives as paid sexual partners—then boasts of it in public—it's not hard to imagine why we can safely say Elagabalus was a Jackass of History.

Unpleasant Trivia...

• If there's two things we can say for sure about Communist dictator Joseph Stalin, it's that he loved having his picture taken, and he was good at making people disappear. He instructed his artists to make sure people disappeared, too. On several occasions, he had artists retouch group photos and paintings, removing his comrades who had been executed or who'd conveniently vanished.

• Caravaggio is one of the great artists of the 16th and 17th centuries. His style is unmistakable, often bringing us weirdly illuminated Biblical scenes. In life, he had a serious anger management problem. At one point, he got into a knife fight with another man over a prostitute. They fought a formal duel, in which Caravaggio, weiling his dagger like a paintbrush, tried to castrate his rival—but he accidentally cut an artery in the man's upper thigh, and was charged with murder. He fled to Malta. The story got out that the fight was over a tennis match, but today we know better.

• Vice-President Andrew Johnson (who later became President when Lincoln was assassinated) took his oath of office while completely wasted. He staggered onto the dais, mumbled something about the Congress, Supreme Court, and the Cabinet owing their positions to "plebeians" like himself, kissed the Bible, and staggered away. Of course, he was later impeached.

• Speaking of Lincoln (who is about as close to a secular saint as a man can get), he didn't much care for the 1st Ammendment. He routinely suppressed freedom of speech and even suspended the inviolable writ of habeas corpus. Like the authors of the Patriot Act much later, he cited "national security" as the end that justified his means.

He was a deeply insecure ruler who pretty much single-handedly ruined the 20th century. When a true jackass like Hitler thinks you're an "idiot," you know you've got serious problems.

KAISER WILHELM II

You're four years old and you're at your uncle's wedding. It's a big deal! Everyone is dressed in their finest. You're a little prince from Germany, sent to England to honor that side of your multinational royal family. They've dressed you up in a little Highlander outfit and even equipped you with a cute little dagger. But royal weddings are long, drawn-out affairs, and after all, you're only four. You get a little antsy and rambunctious, maybe a little noisy. Your 18-year-old uncle (an important fellow who will someday be the Duke of Edinburgh) tells you to knock it off. What does your little four-year-old mind come up with as a response? Threaten him with a dagger. When he tries to take it from you, bite him.

That might sound like the antics of any four-year-old, although most would draw the line at stabbing an adult. But wee little Frederick Wilhelm Victor Albert, Prince of Prussia, did at the wedding of his "Uncle Bertie," the future King Edward VII of England. That little boy was the grandson of Queen Victoria, whose daughter, also Victoria, married the King of Prussia. The King of Prussia was also the Emperor of Germany. When that's your future, maybe even as a four-year-old you think you can take a little license. Either that, or your family suffers from a history of mental illness on both sides, you're an arrogant, obnoxious warmonger, and you grow up to become a Jackass of History.

Kaiser Wilhelm II, the last German monarch, had his good points. He fought to improve conditions for Germany's working class, and to protect women and children from exploitation by industrial interests. He was a patron of the arts and sciences, and reformed Germany's education system. But he was rabidly anti-Jewish, anti-democracy, and believed strongly in aggressive German territorial expansion. He was both jealous of and resentful of his British royal connections, who he felt never accepted him, and he allowed this personal bitterness to inform his foreign policy. He routinely spoke rashly in public, making insensitive statements where tact was required. He was one of the first monarchs of the modern age to humiliate themselves in the press. He was supportive of fascism, and in many ways helped create the conditions for fascism to flourish. Worst of all, his saber-rattling and failed attempts to live up to an idealized, hyper-masculine militaristic tradition led directly to World War I and indirectly to World War II.

It's possible that Wilhelm's attitude might have something to do with deep self-consciousness and low self-esteem. Wilhelm was born with a withered arm due to Erb's Palsy—his left arm was six inches shorter than his right and noticeably less developed. Throughout his life, Wilhelm often successfully diminished or concealed this by using his left arm to grip a saber or cane, much as US Senator Bob Dole would later do with a pencil. Predictably (and appropriately), historians have wondered if this disability had a negative effect on his emotions while growing up. His mother, the daughter of England's Queen Victoria, certainly didn't help by making much of the withered arm. She obsessed over it, blamed herself, and was fixated on the idea that as a future monarch, Wilhelm should be able to ride a horse, but his arm made it terribly difficult for him to keep his balance on a mount. Each day for a period of several weeks during his childhood, she'd force the little prince—often weeping—to practice horseback riding until he could keep his balance. Wilhelm bitterly resented this treatment throughout his whole life, and would later call his mother "a torment."

Wilhelm grew up in the shadow of his grandfather, Kaiser Wilhelm I, who'd (more or less) unified Germany and instituted the so-called Second Reich. Wilhelm hero-worshiped his grandfather and father, but felt distance and resentment toward his mother, who he believed was "too British." He eventually came to see his father as weak and dominated by his mother. Young Wilhelm ignored his mom's advice to learn to respect British-style democracy. Instead, he agreed with the stern, autocratic Prussian tutors his grandfather provided. He later attended university and studied law and politics, becoming immersed in the macho Prussian culture. For the rest of his life, he was rarely photographed without a military uniform. When he turned 21, his grandfather the Kaiser put him in the military, and this made things worse. Trying to prove himself despite (or because of) his withered arm and diminutive stature, Wilhelm's personality—already slightly unpleasant—took a turn for the worse, and he adopted a blunt, barking, indelicate way of dealing with others.

Wilhelm fell under the spell of the "Iron Chancellor," Otto von Bismarck, who managed the day-to-day affairs of running the empire. Bismarck didn't care for

Wilhelm's parents, and he used the young prince as
something of a political weapon against them. Soon
enough Wilhelm became suspicious of his parents, often
accusing them of preferring British interests to German
ones. He blamed his mother for his withered arm
because she allowed only English doctors to treat him.

Wilhelm fell in love with his first cousin, but she
rejected him. He married into the Russian imperial
family instead, and had six sons and a daughter with
Augusta Victoria, a Russian princess. They'd be
married for 40 years and have seven children. Wilhelm's
grandfather thought this connection would set the
young man up for a diplomatic career, and he was sent to
the court of Tsar Alexander III of Russia. Apparently he
made something of an ass of himself there—we're not
sure how, but the Tsar let the Kaiser know he was not
impressed—and a trip planned for England for Queen
Victoria's jubilee was yanked out from under him. This
put him deeper under the control of Bismarck.

The Old Kaiser died, and Wilhelm's father became
Emperor Frederick III—for about 100 days. Then he
died of throat cancer, for which Wilhelm—now at age
29 Kaiser Wilhelm II—blamed his mother (again, for
using English doctors).

If Bismarck thought he was going to push around the
young Emperor, he was wrong. Almost immediately, the
young Kaiser began to push against Bismarck's policies.
One of the most influential men in Europe, Bismarck
favored a cautious, careful, slow-going way to get what
Germany wanted and needed. The new Kaiser was not
blessed with such wisdom or patience. His nickname for
his former mentor was "Old Killjoy." When Bismarck,
a monarchist who hated and feared left-leaning
politics, attempted to pass a draconian anti-Socialist

law, Wilhelm stepped in to get it stopped. Wilhelm instead introduced measures to support working people (although he was far from Socialist). Bismarck then attempted to put together a political coalition to oppose such measures, but when Kaiser Wilhelm found out, he demanded—and got—Bismarck's resignation.

The new Kaiser Wilhelm II wanted Germany to be a world power that would rival England. He, inspired by some of his more warlike Prussian generals, started an aggressive campaign of ship-building, so that Germany would have an invincible navy. This was done openly and with an eye toward making a not-so-veiled threat to British interests. He also had the wisdom to open the Kiel Canal between Denmark and Germany, for faster ship movements from the Baltic to North seas and back again. But his insistence on submarines and huge dreadnought-class warships put a severe financial strain on Germany that only hurt the working class he claimed to champion.

But not everyone agreed with his attitude, and some were worried about his saber-rattling speeches. Most disturbingly and prophetically, Wilhelm would make disparaging remarks about Jews that prove Hitler wasn't exactly reinventing the wheel. A quote: "Let no German...rest until these parasites have been destroyed and exterminated from Germany forever." Another: "[The Jews are] a nuisance that humanity must get rid of some way or other. I believe the best thing would be gas."

As for his foreign policy, the word that best describes it, in hindsight, is "disastrous." At a time when Germany needed to be on good terms with England, Wilhelm publicly praised the president of the Transvaal Republic for standing up to the British, which alienated the

Kaiser from his British relatives. He also spent a great deal of time and effort spreading fear of what he called the "Yellow Peril," predicting that Japan and China would team up and conquer Western Europe. His attempts to strengthen German colonies in Africa and the Pacific were complete failures, and in Africa led to the near-complete genocide of two ethnic groups (though, to be fair, Wilhelm did eventually order a stop to this). He brutally crushed Arab rebels in 1889, and when Germany sent troops to aid the British in the Boxer Rebellion in China, he offended even his die-hard Prussian warmongers by insisting they take no prisoners and ordering them to be "merciless to the Chinese." After all that, German troops showed up late, after the British and Japanese had already won. It was diplomatically embarrassing, and state censors would later remove his exhortations to eschew mercy from the written record.

Kaiser Wilhelm's worst public relations blunder by far was an interview he granted to the British newspaper the Daily Telegraph. He made ridiculous claims that deeply offended the British. He intended to use the interview to promote relations between England and Germany, but allowed himself several emotional outbursts during the interview, saying, "The English are mad, mad as March Hares," accusing the French and British of trying to incite Germany to violence in Africa, saying the "German people care nothing for England," and coyly implying that the massive naval build-up he ordered was in response to fears of Japanese aggression, rather than to rival the British—a statement so obviously disingenuous that even Germans were embarrassed by it. By the time the interview hit Germany, there were loud calls for Wilhelm's abdication. He laid low for a while, then blamed his chancellor, Bernhard von Bulow, for not censoring the interview before it was published (which Bulow had no authority to do in Germany and no ability to do in England or elsewhere).

He was a close friend of Franz Ferdinand, Archduke of Austria, whose assassination by a terrorist/rebel group called The Black Hand led to the First World War. Blaming the Serbians, Austria-Hungary declared war on them. Kaiser Wilhelm immediately supported the effort, and declared war on Russia when Russia declared war on Austria-Hungary in defense of Serbia. Kaiser Wilhelm blamed the situation on a vast, intricate conspiracy between Russia, France and England to provoke Germany into war (because of its treaties with Austria-Hungary) for the sole purpose of starting a war of aggression against Germany.

Unfortunately, once the war started it became evident that Kaiser Wilhelm's generals essentially ignored him and did as they wished. Field Marshall Hindenburg and General Ludendorff wanted a swift move against France, which they thought would be easy pickings. They ignored Wilhelm's request to invade Russia first, although both approaches were designed to prevent a two-front war. The military charged into France through Belgium, provoking war with England, and then got bogged down in trench warfare in France, and kept at it even when it was obvious the strategy wasn't working.

In fact, word got out that the German military was ignoring Kaiser Wilhelm to the point that US President Woodrow Wilson publicly stated that it would be pointless to negotiate a treaty with the Kaiser, as he had no significant control over the military. Meanwhile, he was so unpopular that there were popular uprisings against him in Berlin, and the Navy ultimately (and officially) mutinied, throwing off his command. He was shocked by these betrayals, and recalled bitterly that Bismarck had warned him what would happen if Wilhelm's saber-rattling gave too much power to the military.

Fearing for his life, Wilhelm fled by train to the Netherlands. After the Treaty of Versailles ended the war in 1919, he was sought for prosecution as a war criminal. But Woodrow Wilson put a stop to this, saying it would do no good to punish Wilhelm and jeopardize peace. Safely settled in a country house in the Netherlands, Wilhelm formally abdicated. The new Weimar Republic allowed him to remove nearly 30 train cars of his furniture and personal effects to his new home.

In the Netherlands, Wilhelm grew out his beard, learned Dutch, entertained, and became a pretty good amateur archeologist, a hobby which fascinated him. He also developed a weird obsession with chopping wood—huge piles of it were all over his estate—and drawing pictures of battleships and public buildings he still hoped to design if the German monarchy were ever restored. In fact, he vowed never to return to Germany until that happened, even if he wasn't the monarch. When the Nazis came to power, he hoped they would restore him, or at least his grandson, in the role of Kaiser. But Hitler knew public opinion blamed Wilhelm for Germany's defeat in World War I, and ignored him. Wilhelm, despite his anti-Semitism, actually spoke out against the Kristallnacht campaign of terror and violence against Jews and anti-Nazis, saying he was, for the first time, "ashamed to be a German." Nevertheless, he was enough of a jackass to send Hitler a letter that read: "My Fuhrer, I congratulate you and hope that under your marvelous leadership, the German monarchy will be restored completely."

Hitler's response: "What an idiot." Poking the
bear, Wilhelm later sent Hitler a letter saying
"Congratulations, you are victorious with my troops."
However, when the Nazis conquered the Netherlands
in 1940, Wilhelm was wise enough to retire from public
life and keep his mouth shut. Winston Churchill, prime
minister of England, actually offered to let Wilhelm
take refuge in England for the remainder of the war, but
Wilhelm refused, saying he preferred to die at home.
The Nazis put an honor guard outside his house, which
irritated Hitler. But when Wilhelm died at 82, just a few
weeks before Germany invaded Russia, Hitler wanted
to bring his body back for a state funeral, hoping to link
the Nazi regime with the historical Reich, but this never
happened. A small state funeral was instead provided in
the Netherlands, with Wilhelm's final request—that no
swastiksas or other Nazi regalia would be present at his
funeral—purposely ignored.

Wilhelm left behind a slim autobiography, and this
damns him more than any jackassery he got up to in life.
He spent many pages explaining why World War I was
not his fault—it was, he said, the fault of Freemasons
and Jews. He said the Jews secretly started World War II.
He wrote that Germany was "the land of monarchy and
Christ," while England was "the land of liberalism, and
therefore of Satan." He said he admired England but that
it had fallen from greatness, and that that "the British
people must be liberated from Antichrist Judah."

Are there bigger Jackasses of History? Absolutely.
But in terms of personal bitterness leading indirectly to
two devastating world wars, Kaiser Wilhelm II certainly
deserves his spot on the list.

He figured out an aggressive way to make himself King of Scotland. But when you rape your way to the top, you won't stay there long—in fact, you'll die insane in a Danish prison.

JAMES HEPBURN, EARL OF BOTHWELL

Let's return to the court of Mary, Queen of Scots—a veritable circus of jackassery. James Hepburn, the 4th Earl of Bothwell (we'll call him Bothwell) was Mary's third husband. He was a bombastic, confident, brusque, take-charge fellow. After Mary's first two husbands —both weak and immature men—he must have seemed like a breath of fresh air. But he wasn't. While Mary was enough of a jackass that she would have fallen from grace eventually, Bothwell didn't help delay that day. In fact he hurried it along.

Bothwell was born into nobility, and by the time he'd grown up, he was the Lord High Admiral of Scotland. One of his first jobs was to sail around Europe trying to garner military support for Scotland against England. This was a good job for Bothwell. He was a staunch nationalist who feared the rising power of Protestant lords in Scotland. He saw this as the first step to eventual union with England, a prospect he and several other important Scottish interests saw as the End of the World.

In a perfect example of "what comes around, goes around," Bothwell sealed his fate early by the ill-treatment of his first wife, but it would take decades for her to get her well-deserved revenge. While visiting the courts of Europe on his mission, he stopped in Copenhagen to negotiate with King Frederick II of Denmark. There, he met Anna, the lovely young daughter of a Norwegian admiral who was posted in Denmark. Very quickly, they were married. Bothwell would later claim that under Scottish law, they were never technically married, but according to Norwegian law, they most definitely were. Bothwell certainly had no qualms about accepting a rather large dowry, which he promptly wasted.

Stuck in Flanders, having squandered his new wife's money, Bothwell compelled her to sell most of her fine possessions. She did. When that money ran out, Bothwell sent her home to beg money from her family. While there, she complained to her parents of Bothwell's terrible treatment of her, and the two eventually went their separate ways—that is, she stayed home and he never tried to collect her. Bothwell went on to France, where he'd meet his doom, Mary, Queen of Scots.

Mary was a child queen of Scotland who'd been raised in France as the teenage wife of young King Francis. He died young, and she was returned to Scotland, not really fitting in and causing scandal at every turn. Meanwhile, her mother, Mary of Guise, a French noblewoman, ran Scotland. Bothwell helped her out in several struggles with Protestant lords, and was so taken with her daughter that he found three separate occasions to return to the French court. The impressionable young Mary showered him with money and political appointments. When Francis died and she was sent home, Bothwell organized and captained her naval escort.

Mary lost no time in alienating her new Scottish

subjects, though she certainly had her favorites. She married the hapless idiot Lord Darnley—only after his minions had carried out an assassination against one of her chief supporters (and probably lovers). They tried to get Bothwell, too, but he escaped. For whatever reason, she married Darnley, whose behavior became so erratic and insufferable that she quickly regretted it. He only did one thing right—got her pregnant with little James, who would eventually succeed his cousin Elizabeth I as the ruler of England. But that's another story.

Meanwhile, Bothwell, deciding he was not actually married to the Norwegian Anna, married Jean Gordon, a nobleman's daughter. And yet he gave the first dance at his wedding to Mary—a breach of etiquette that did not go unnoticed. His marriage to Gordon lasted only a year—she left him and petitioned the Catholic church for a divorce on the grounds of adultery. Apparently Bothwell had been sleeping with her servant.

When her baby James was just a few days old, Mary heard that Bothwell had been wounded and was near death. Apparently he'd taken it on himself to track down and arrest a notorious outlaw, John Elliot, a bandit leader and cattle rustler, was unsuccessful, and been wounded. Her flight to his side raised lots of eyebrows and began rumors that they were more than just friends. Snippets of love letters between them, found centuries later among the papers of the English ambassador to Scotland, seem to confirm this.

At any rate, it wasn't long after that Lord Darnley's house conveniently exploded—leaving Mary free to marry again. She arranged for a deputation of loyal nobles to sign a bill declaring that she must marry a native-born Scotsman.

Darnley's murder was no mystery according to most,

who thought Bothwell did it. He was already known as a loudmouth and a troublemaker at court—earlier, he'd argued with the Earl of Arran so fiercely that he was briefly imprisoned for it—and opinion was widespread that Bothwell was responsible for Darnley's murder, likely with the full connivance of the Queen. He was formally accused by the Privy Council, and, after a trial, he was acquitted of murder charges. But there was serious pressure from the top, and the trial's result was so distrusted by the populace that the Queen felt obliged to ride to Parliament a week later, with Bothwell, who was obviously and provocatively holding the King's Sceptre. She cajoled Parliament into declaring that Bothwell's trial was just (which probably wouldn't have been necessary if it had been).

A few days later, Mary was on the road to Edinburgh with her escort, but Bothwell rode up with 800 men and told her Edinburgh wasn't safe. She should come to Dunbar Castle, he said, where she could take refuge from the non-existent threat. Whether this was a "kidnapping" or part of a plan between Bothwell and Mary, we'll never know. Once at Dunbar Castle, Bothwell is said to have held the queen captive and raped her to secure marriage to her. However, historians are split down the middle when it comes to Mary's complicity in all this. Her recorded behavior leaves us good reasons to doubt that he was kidnapped or forced without her consent, and modern sensibilities, revisiting history from the perspective of women's studies, would have you believe she was a victim. Truth is, we'll never know.

However, if Bothwell did kidnap and rape her, that didn't stop her from naming him a Duke and a Marquis, gifting him with a fabulously expensive fur-lined nightgown, and marrying him just a few days later. She issued a formal statement saying that while she may have appeared to have been forced, she was exercising her own will. But the Protestant lords who had always opposed her, now joined by some Catholic lords who realized they'd probably be better off without her as long as she was attracted to jackasses like Darnley and Bothwell, signed a proclamation denouncing the Queen and her new beau.

Battle lines were drawn—literally—and within a month two armies, one for the Queen and Bothwell, one for Parliament, met at Carberry Hill. The "rebels" flew a banner depicting the murdered Darnley. It soon became apparent that Mary's troops were disinclined to actually fight for her, after making an initial show of force. Bothwell dramatically challenged Baron William Kirkcaldy to single combat to decide the affair, but when Kirkcaldy gladly accepted, Bothwell backed down, mumbling some feeble excuse about how he couldn't fight Kirkcaldy after all, because he was only a baron and Bothwell was a duke.

Kirkcaldy told the Queen if she'd send Bothwell away, they'd be loyal to her and escort her to Edinburgh, where she would *definitely not* be thrown in prison. Perhaps disillusioned with Bothwell, she agreed, and he was too happy to rush off the field with some 25 men after a final quick hug and kiss for Mary (they never saw one another again). Seeing this, Mary's troops surrendered. Mary was captured and *definitely was* thrown into prison. She complained of seeing Darnley's face on her enemies' banner, and they taunted her by hanging it right outside her cell window. She was 24 and her life was basically over. She abdicated the throne in favor of her infant son, who she never saw again, either. She'd eventually flee to England seeking Queen Elizabeth's help, but Elizabeth saw her as a threat, kept her closely confined and watched for a few more decades, then cut her head off when she wouldn't stop conspiring to replace Elizabeth.

Meanwhile, after the "battle," Bothwell obtained a ship and fled to the Shetlands—a group of islands just northeast of Scotland. There, he tried to hire German mercenaries. But Kirkcaldy was in hot pursuit, and after a three-hour sea battle, a storm blew in. Kirkcaldy's ship ran aground, and Bothwell escaped, but the storm forced him to sail to Norway. There, he was arrested for not having the right commercial shipping papers (red tape, even back then!).

Now is when Anna, his first wife, got her revenge. Jackass that he was, when he was arrested, he dropped her name, useful for its important family connections, in a bid to get out of prison. But Anna ignored him, and wouldn't speak up for him. In fact, she sued him for spousal abandonment, for the recovery of her wasted dowry, and for his squandering of her possessions during their marriage. Bothwell was sent to prison in Copenhagen, but the Danish King Frederick II didn't really know what to do with him. The king held onto Bothwell for a while as a potential political bargaining chip, but it soon became clear that Mary was never going to be the Queen of Scotland, England, or anywhere else ever again. Rather than letting Bothwell go, Frederick decided to send the Scotsman to the notorious hell-hole Dragsholm Castle.

At Dragsholm, a favorite place to hide away political dissidents, Bothwell was essentially forgotten. Frederick had already publicly opined that he believed Bothwell was insane. If he wasn't before, his decade in Dragsholm—known for terrible conditions— definitely drove Bothwell stark-raving mad. Today, visitors to Dragsholm (which is now a hotel and dining establishment!) can still see the post Bothwell was chained to for 10 years, and they can even see the groove in the floor where Bothwell walked around and around in circles for a decade, ranting and raving and forgotten. He died there in 1578, some nine years before Mary's eventual execution.

So, once again, we see that Mary, Queen of Scots, was partial to jackasses. But she had her marriage to Bothwell annulled in 1570, in the hope that some European Catholic monarch would still marry her and catapult her to the English throne. And Bothwell, jackass that he was, died insane and alone, for the love of a flighty, impetuous, arrogant, easily dominated jackass of a queen who very quickly forgot all about him.

Unpleasant Trivia...

• Peter the Great was the emperor of Russia for 40 years, and in the late 17th and early 18th centuries, started an economic and cultural renaissance that brought Russia into line with the rest of Europe. Plenty of nasty stories about Peter the Great are out there. One is that, although he'd regularly squeeze the breasts of his wife's ladies-in-waiting, even when she was in the room, he wasn't as forgiving of her indiscretions. When she had an affair with William Mons, the brother of one of Peter's mistresses, he cut off Mons' head, preserved it in a jar, and had it displayed in his wife's bedroom for the rest of their marriage.

• By the time Adolph Hitler was elected Chancellor of Germany in 1934, he owed about 405,500 reichsmarks in back taxes (about $6.3 million in today's dollars). A tax official who could see which way the wind was blowing forgave him this debt, and was rewarded with a tax-free allowance of 2,000 reichsmarks a month "for life." By comparison, teachers makde about 4,800 reichsmarks a year.

Rising from poverty to hobnob with the rich and famous, she was a skilled and sexy confidence trickster who tried to pull a scam on the French royalty—and almost got away with it.

JEANNE DE VALOIS

Men aren't the only Jackasses of History. Plenty of women can claim that dubious title, as well. Let's meet one—the beautiful, greedy Jeanne de Valois. She was a confidence artist who exploited her charisma and good looks to rise from poverty to pulling off the con of the century against Marie Antoinette and the French royal court—and she almost got away with it.

Jeanne was born in 1756 to a very poor family, but a family that clung to a decayed noble line. Her father, Jacques de Valois de Saint-Remy, was descended from an illegitimate child of Henry II of France, who lived some two hundred years earlier. Though he was known to have noble blood, Jacques was also known as a drunk who squandered his money and neglected his children to a degree we'd find criminal today. Jeanne's mother was a servant girl said by contemporaries to be "debauched" and "dissolute." In some ways, Jeanne would turn out a lot like her mother. In the meantime, she and her two siblings, a brother and sister, were regular characters in the town of Bar-sur-Aube, where they dressed in rags, went barefoot, tended cows and did other odd jobs, and begged for food. They were often locked out of their house for days at a time. This early poverty had a deep and lasting impression on Jeanne.

Eventually, the de Valois kids met a kindly priest, who

thought it sad that children should suffer so—children descended from nobility, that is—and he moved them to Boulogne, near Paris, where a court determined that they indeed had royal ancestry and should not live in poverty. Ironically, although France was in terrible financial turmoil during this time, a fund existed to remedy this very problem (there being, apparently, hundreds of descendants of the illegitimate offspring of nobles crowding the streets of Paris). The children were given yearly stipends from this fund. Jeanne's brother was given a post in the army (he later died in battle). She and her sister were sent to a boarding school known for producing scores of future nuns.

But the nun's life was not for young Jeanne, who was said by contemporaries to be strikingly beautiful, with a charming smile, a "regal, small-breasted figure" and "the wiles of a Circe." Finishing school, she and her sister did not enter a nunnery as arranged, but instead went back home to Bar-sur-Aube and took up residence with an important family, the Surmonts. Soon, her sister decided to live the religious life, took up her nun's habit, and disappears from history. Jeanne, on the other hand, set her sights on Surmont's roguish nephew, Nicolas de la Motte. He was a gendarme, or police officer, and was, even at this early stage, probably not the shining example of a "good cop," as he was friendly with numerous forgers, prostitutes, and other petty criminals. Soon enough, a heavily pregnant Jeanne married Nicolas, and gave birth to twins a month later. Sadly, the twins died after only a few days.

Like Jeanne's family, the de la Motte family also claimed to have noble blood, but that claim was tenuous at best. Nevertheless, the young couple styled themselves the Comte and Comtesse (that is, Count and

Countess) de la Motte, and jumped into a lavish lifestyle that was far beyond their means. Perhaps because of her childhood poverty, or perhaps from simple greed (or a bit of both), Jeanne had a desperate desire to live richly. It soon became obvious to her that Nicolas was not going to be able to provide such a life.

In those days, any citizen who was properly dressed was allowed to visit the royal palace at Versailles and hope to get a glimpse of the royal family—in this case, the young King Louis XVI and his Austrian bride, Marie Antoinette. Jeanne intended to arrange to casually meet the Queen and ask for her annual stipend to be increased (she thought that as a woman, the Queen would be easier to deal with). However, Marie Antoinette had heard disturbing rumors about Jeanne's lifestyle, and, already battling a bad reputation with the public, refused to see her.

These rumors about Jeanne's dissolute lifestyle were true. By this time she had taken a lover, with the full blessing and connivance of Nicolas. His friend, Retaux de Vilette, was a fellow corrupt officer of the gendarmes, a master forger, and a gigolo who was well-skilled at obtaining large regular gifts of cash from his elderly patrons. He became Jeanne's lover, and the three engaged in a semi-open *menage-a-trois* relationship. All three were ambitious and attractive, and had all the tools necessary to be incredible con artists—which, thanks to a new man in Jeanne's life, they'd soon become.

Jeanne's incursions into Versailles gave her occasion to meet the powerful Cardinal Prince Louis de Rohan, a noble and high-ranking official in the Catholic Church. Cardinal Rohan had opposed the idea of marriage between King Louis XVI and Marie Antoinette, and the Queen never forgave him for it. She also thought his lifestyle to be hypocritical and venial, if not outright evil. It seems he was more dumb than evil, however. Using her "wiles of a Circe," Jeanne quickly ingratiated herself with Cardinal Rohan, becoming his mistress, but more importantly, his confidante. It soon became clear to Jeanne that Cardinal Rohan was desperate to get back into Marie Antoinette's good graces, and that furthermore, he harbored something of a sexual obsession with her—but from a distance, as the Queen rarely deigned to be in the same parlor or banqueting hall with him.

Cardinal Rohan made regular gifts of cash to Jeanne, and secured for her husband Nicolas a much better-paying job in the prestigious bodyguard of the nobleman the Comte d'Artois. Of course, none of this was enough to satisfy her ambition for more wealth. Little did Jeanne know, all she had to do was wait, and Cardinal Rohan would become one prong of a conspiracy to make her wealthy beyond her dreams.

The other prong came when a famous jeweler, Boehmer, made news as he tried to sell a fabulously expensive diamond necklace. It had been ordered by Louis XVI's father for his mistress, Madame du Barry, but he'd died before it was completed. Neither Louis XVI or Marie Antoinette cared for Madame du Barry, and had already ensured she'd been sent far from court. Now, Boehmer was stuck without a buyer for the necklace. He'd invested a fortune in it, scouring Europe for years to find large enough diamonds. In very real danger of financial ruin, he approached Louis XVI and Marie Antoinette to ask if they would buy it (in fact, they were one of the few people in France who could afford it). But Marie, not wishing to wear jewelry created for another woman—especially one she hated—turned

Boehmer down.

When Jeanne got wind of this, various puzzle pieces began to click together in her mind. Together, she, Nicolas, and de Villette formed a conspiracy to enrich themselves, using Boehmer's desperation and Cardinal Rohan's obsession with Marie Antoinette as their weapons. de Villette, with his forger's skills, faked a series of letters from Marie to Jeanne that illustrated a deep trust between the two. One of the letters indicated that Marie would have loved to purchase the necklace, but that Louis XVI was loathe to make such an extravagant purchase while France was in debt and facing financial ruin. Marie, already known as "Madame Deficit" for her irresponsibly lavish spending sprees, made this lie more believable by her own behavior. The letters asked Jeanne to act as the secret liaison between Marie and Cardinal Rohan. de Villette then forged letters from the Queen to the Cardinal himself, implying that her distaste for him was merely a defense mechanism against the love she felt for him. She asked him, as personal favor, to secretly lend her the money to buy the necklace.

Blinded by his own desires and the egging-on of his lovely but conniving young mistress, Cardinal Rohan swallowed the whole thing hook, line and sinker. He agreed to buy the necklace for the Queen, but he had a condition first—he insisted on a late-night secret rendezvous with the Queen. This was supposedly done on the advice of the so-called "Count Cagliostro," a self-proclaimed mystic and holy man who specialized in selling "magical Egyptian amulets." He was actually an Italian adventurer fleeing the Inquisition.

Jeanne was stymied at first—how would she arrange the illicit rendezvous Rohan wanted? Luckily, the conspiracy's go-to guy, de Villette, knew a prostitute named Nicole le Guay d'Olivia. Nicole had made a decent living for herself because of her startling resemblance to Marie Antoinette, whom she would often impersonate for her clients. Jeanne arranged the secret late-night assignation, and Rohan spent some time privately with Nicole, believing her to be the Queen, doing who-knows-what.

Cardinal Rohan was all too happy to get the necklace, and sent an agent to collect it from Boehmer on promise of later payment. Boehmer, himself in dire straits, agreed to the deal, believing he was selling the necklace to the Queen through Rohan, so the Queen could avoid scandal. The Cardinal immediately gave the necklace to Jeanne, who was supposed to deliver it to Marie Antoinette. Instead, she gave it to Nicolas, who secretly left France, went to London, and began selling off the diamonds one-by-one.

But it was soon time for Cardinal Rohan to pay Boehmer, through Jeanne as intermediary. When she arrived with the funds, Boehmer was horrified—it was not enough, not the price he thought he'd agreed on. It is assumed that Jeanne had pocketed the difference at some point, but it's also possible Cardinal Rohan was trying to stiff Boehmer. At any rate, it was a mistake— Boehmer went directly to the King and Queen to complain about what he thought was their failure to pay.

Marie Antoinette was outraged—she said she didn't want the necklace, never ordered it, and never received it. At this point the disconsolate Boehmer told the whole story of his negotiations with Rohan through Jeanne. The King and Queen staged a public rebuke for the Cardinal. Waiting until the Feast of the Annunciation, a religious festival the Cardinal was to officiate, Louis XVI demanded before the entire court that the Cardinal explain himself. Flustered, afraid and embarrassed, Rohan produced one of the forged letters to prove his case. Unfortunately, the letters were signed with Marie Antoinette's full name. This was the conspirators' tragic mistake: French royalty, by long-standing tradition, never signed their full names to anything—only their given names. Louis believed that Rohan had been fooled, but this didn't stop his rage. Louis was scandalized that someone with such an important position could have been fooled so easily, and he told Rohan he should have known how the royalty of France signed their correspondence. Rohan was immediately arrested and sent to the Bastille, where he told all.

Over the next few days, authorities rounded up and arrested de Villette, Jeanne, the prostitute Nicole, and the occultist Cagliostro (who was only peripherally involved, but the court wanted him out of the way). Of course, Jeanne's husband escaped arrest because he was out of the country selling the diamonds! It took the King's men a few days to catch Jeanne, and by that time she'd destroyed the letters, costumes and other evidence of the plot.

All for naught, of course—de Villette squealed like a pig and sang like a canary under interrogation, as did Nicole. They implicated Jeanne and Nicolas as the prime movers in the affair. Rohan, cooling his heels in the Bastille, agreed to be tried by the Parliament of Paris as his judges. Louis XVI and Marie Antoinette insisted on a public trial, because word had gotten out, and with Marie's already-poor reputation as a profligate spender, they wanted to be sure they were exonerated in the eyes of the people. Pope Pius VI was miffed, and wrote letters to the King saying the Cardinal should be tried in a church court. The Pope's letters went unanswered, as far as we know.

When the trial came, Louis XVI and Marie Antoinette made sure it was open to the public and well-covered by the scandal-sheets of the day—it was the 18th century equivalent of a media circus. But the King and Queen were shocked when the court acquitted Cardinal Rohan, saying his only crime was being too naive. They also acquitted the prostitute Nicole. de Villette got off somewhat easy, being exiled from France. Cagliostro was exiled as well (and was soon captured by the Inquisition to meet a sorry fate). Nicolas was convicted *in absentia*, but he was safe in London. Jeanne got the worst of it. She was publicly flogged, then branded on both shoulders with a "V"—the first letter of the French word for thief—and thrown into a prison for prostitutes.

Unfortunately, the public nature of the trial completely backfired. When the court acquitted Rohan, who was well-known to be hated by Marie Antoinette, it was seen as something of a rebuke against the Queen, who'd pushed for his public trial. To make matters worse, she convinced the king to exile Rohan, too, despite his acquittal. This abuse of executive power, plus the other acquittals, gave the public the impression that the entire affair had been orchestrated by Marie Antoinette, and that poor Jeanne was just a convenient scapegoat. The public was all too ready to believe the worst of their foreign queen.

Perhaps this helps explain how Jeanne, after about a year in prison, managed to cut her hair, obtain the clothing of a peasant lad, and escape the prison disguised as a boy. She fled France and made her way to England, where she joined Nicolas in London. There, she and Nicolas lived off the proceeds of the diamond sales, presumably. But even that wasn't enough to support Jeanne's extreme lifestyle. She soon amassed a large quantity of debt to English creditors. She made some money through the sale of her autobiography, in which she protested her innocence and said she had been tricked and abandoned by Marie Antoinette, who she named as the author of the conspiracy. But money from book sales was never enough.

Nevertheless, it seemed Jeanne had won—or at least gotten away with it. But justice is sometimes delayed and ironic. On a hot summer day in 1791, Jeanne's creditors stormed the expensive hotel she was staying at. In an attempt to hide from them, she tried to climb out her hotel window to take refuge on a ledge or balcony (the record is unclear). According to extant reports in *The Times*, Jeanne fell from the window, plummeting to the street where she writhed for a bit, then died. One of her eyes was smashed out, both of her legs were broken, and the newspapers referred to her body as "mangled."

Two years later, Marie Antoinette would find herself on the wrong end of a guillotine blade during the French Revolution. Even today, some historians think maybe Marie was behind the plot after all, but most lay the blame squarely on the shoulders of the ambitious, hypersexual con artist Jeanne de Valois, our first female Jackass of History.

Unpleasant Trivia...

• Nicola Tesla was a brilliant scientist and inventor. He did important early research into Alternating Current, X-rays, and, most importantly, radio. He also believed that the mentally ill, handicapped, and criminals should be systematically removed via forced tubal ligations, vasectomies, hysterectomies, castration and abortion. What a guy!

He had shifting convictions and his ambition was extreme. From stabbing classmates to bombing Ethiopia, he was a bully at heart who fought his way to the top—and back down again.

BENITO MUSSOLINI

He wanted to restore the glory of Ancient Rome to Italy, but his ship of state would crash on the titanic iceberg of his own ego. Meet Benito Mussolini—a dynamic speaker and charismatic leader who also happened to be a complete Jackass of History.

In Mussolini's case, the evidence of his jackassery stacks up early in life. Attending services with his Socialist parents at the local Catholic church, young Mussolini was fond of waiting for mass, then, with the congregants kneeling and close-eyed, pinching them as hard as he could and then moving his hand away quickly. Nevertheless, he got caught a few times and the priest asked Mr. and Mrs. Mussolini if they'd kindly keep their kid under control. Little did anyone know these youthful hijinks were the first sparks of a lifelong flame of violence.

When he was 10 years old, Mussolini was expelled from Catholic school for stabbing a classmate. We don't know the details, but we can safely assume it was Mussolini's fault. Sent to another parochial school, he stabbed another classmate there. As a teen, he stabbed his girlfriend in the arm. He also led an unruly gang of boys who conducted night-time raids on poor farmers, during which time he became, in the eyes of his contemporaries, a "master swordsman."

Eventually, however, Mussolini settled enough to earn good grades and graduate. Facing extreme poverty in Italy—and the possibility of compulsory military service—he moved to Switzerland in 1902. Here, he wrote eloquently promoting Socialism, although he was unable to find a "real" job anywhere. He studied and improved the fiery rhetorical style he'd later become known for. Mussolini soon ran afoul of Swiss authorities, however, when he openly advocated a violent worker's strike. He was arrested for not having legal immigration papers and deported back to Italy. For some reason, they let him out of prison even though he'd fled military service, and he went right back to Switzerland. While studying there, he was arrested again for forging immigration papers, and sent back to Italy. This time, he stayed, because the Italian government was offering amnesties for military deserters if they spent two years in the army. This he did, and after his service became a schoolteacher.

But teaching school didn't satisfy Mussolini's ambition. He left Italy again to move to Austria, where he did office work for the Socialist Party, moonlighting by writing inflammatory articles for Socialist newspapers. Austrian authorities were not amused, and expelled him from the country for his critiques of nationalism and militarism—an odd stance for a future Fascist.

Back in Italy, he became the editor of a popular Socialist newspaper, wrote numerous other Socialist pieces for other publications, and published a novel that was a not-so-thinly veiled attack on organized religion, particularly Roman Catholicism. All of this raised his clout among left-leaning types, and he was considered to be one of the most prominent members of the Socialist movement in Italy.

Then came World War I. The Socialists were opposed to it. But Mussolini was changing. Perhaps it was the fires of his inner rages that never quite dampened. Regardless of how one feels about organized Socialism, one can't deny that one of the basic tenets of the movement is egalitarianism. Mussolini, on the contrary, began to identify with Nietzche's concept of the "superman." He felt the Socialist movement was too weak, and could benefit from some of Nietzhe's philosophy. Socialists in Italy by and large opposed the war, but Mussolini seems to have seen it as a springboard for his personal ambition. After some anti-military demonstrators were killed by police, the party formally came out against the war. At first, Mussolini agreed, but soon switched his stance. He openly supported the war, saying it would free Italians living in Austria-Hungary from their long-standing submission to old-world nobility such as the Habsburgs and Hohenzollerns. He believed repressing what he called "reactionary" regimes through the war would enhance conditions for Italy's working class.

Needless to say, he was expelled from the party. Whether it was bitterness, his always-simmering anger, or for some other reason, Mussolini began an energetic campaign of support for the war, staging several demonstrations that turned violent. He began to espouse the idea that a "vanguard of revolutionary elites" should lead society, citing Plato's *Republic* as his main influence. He rejected his former opposition to nationalism almost overnight, opting instead for bellicose statements about the former glory of Rome and how Italy might use the war to return to that power. He started a new newspaper to support the war and the nascent, as-yet-unformed concept of Fascism. Surprise, surprise, the newspaper was funded by an Italian arms manufacturer.

Say what you will of him (and I will) but Mussolini at least backed up his words with actions. He joined the army and spent some nine months in hellish trench warfare conditions. He was wounded when a mortar exploded near him, riddling his body with 40 pieces of shrapnel. He was given the rank of corporal, and his superiors spoke highly of him.

As one historian has said, the Mussolini that returned from the war was not the same Mussolini who went into it. He came out of it convinced that Socialism was a failure, and that pragmatic solutions to political problems transcended the burdens of morality—in other words, he came to espouse a policy of political violence. Fascists were a disorganized lot—and didn't go by that name at first—but Mussolini officially started a new part for them: The Facsisti. He used his charisma and eloquence to band the disparate Fascists together into a strong national party. Known as Blackshirts, they used violence on their political enemies, beating and murdering some, forcing others to drink Castor oil, and destroying property. Oddly, the Italian authorities did nothing to curb this violence.

The Italian King, Victor Emmanuel III, appears to have been a little afraid of Mussolini. One night Mussolini led his supporters in a "March on Rome" and demanded to be made Prime Minister. The King agreed. It seems the King feared civil war, and knowing that Mussolini was popular among the military and the working class, thought he could bring order to Italy. He didn't count on Mussolini being able to stage an effective coup and establish a totalitarian regime—but that's exactly what happened.

Mussolini kept up the pretense of democracy for a long time, but worked the system to declare him dictator for one year (there was a legal precedent for this). Once in power, he ousted most of the other political parties from the Italian government and put Fascists in all the key posts. Despite having the appearance of being friendly to the working class, he passed legislation that favored wealthy industrial barons and aristocrats while disbanding or curtailing most labor unions.

He also began to talk openly about Italy's right to annex lands adjoining the Mediterranean Sea. Much like Hitler's concept of "living space," Mussolini spoke of Italy needing "vital space." He said the fact that Italy was overpopulated proved that its people had shown their Darwinistic superiority over other cultures. He advocated the invasion of Slavic and African nations based on their racial and cultural inferiority to Italians. He put this to the test when Greece and Albania were having a border dispute. They sought outside help from the League of Nations to adjudicate it, who sent an Italian general. When that general was murdered (either by pro-Greek forces or bandits), Mussolini responded by sending the Italian Navy to the Greek island of Corfu. There, the navy bombarded the island for 30 solid minutes—and didn't kill a single soldier. Instead, Mussolini instructed the navy to bombard only refugee centers. The vast majority of those killed were children.

Desperate to form a settlement, the League of Nations stepped in, but Mussolini dominated and abused the proceedings, demanding huge reparation payments from Greece, which the League lamely acquiesced to. In the end, Greece was left with a financial depression and Mussolini had a toehold in the Adriatic Sea. The situation was far more complex than it sounds, and what it really proved was that the League of Nations was utterly incompetent when it came to a strong nation abusing a weak one, and the world saw that Mussolini openly thumbed his nose at the League without repercussions.

Soon Mussolini dropped all pretenses of democracy. His regime faced upcoming elections, so he sent his Blackshirts out into the streets to conduct intimidation at the polls, which worked. But one Socialist leader, Giacomo Matteotti, was assassinated for speaking out against Blackshirt interference in the elections. Mussolini tried to hush this up, but too many witnesses saw it. Public opinion began to go against Mussolini and the Fascists. Socialist-led anti-Fascist demonstrations were gaining support. At this point the Fascist leaders told Mussolini that if he didn't put down the socialists, they'd do it for him. Rather than let his underlings take over, Mussolini formally abolished the old government and set himself up as Il Duce, "the leader," as absolute ruler.

What followed was a period with the strange dichotomy of the formation of a totalitarian police state with laws that attempted to fix the economy, as well as public works programs to alleviate unemployment— another "about face" for Il Duce. He also promoted new farming practices that, in general, resulted in short-term successes but long-term problems, because the program was run so inefficiently that it actually put the government into debt. Mussolini encouraged citizens to melt down their gold and give it to the government in exchange for metal bracelets with a patriotic slogans. He also began one of history's most effective "Cult of Personality" campaigns, which attributed to him quasi-divine qualities. He personally selected all newspaper editors and reorganized the schools to indoctrinate Italian children with Fascist philosophy. In another obvious "about face," he signed a deal with the Catholic Church, in which the Pope formally recognized Mussolini's regime, Vatican City would remain supposedly free from interference, and Mussolini promised to "punish the Pope's enemies." This led many Roman Catholics to support Mussolini—not just in Italy, but around the world.

Mussolini believed that, as Hitler rose to power and a second war looked likely, that Italy could "swing" the balance of power in Europe by joining one side or the other. He concluded that the price for Italy's alliance would be support for Mussolini's dream of empire in the African and Slavic nations. Seeing England and France as the chief bar to this, he actually drew up plans for an invasion of France in 1933. But French intelligence officers managed to decrypt Mussolini's communications for a surprise attack, and he abandoned the plan. Then, realizing that Hitler's rise potentially threatened Italy's interest in conquering Slavic peoples, Mussolini sought an alliance with England, France, and Germany in order to keep Hitler in check. He even threatened to go to war with Germany if it invaded Austria. But all that changed in the blink of an eye with Mussolini's invasion of Ethiopia.

Historians differ about why Mussolini chose to attack Ethiopia. Although many European powers had colonies in Africa and elsewhere, by the 1930s the feeling against European colonialism was at a high, even in Europe. It's possible that Mussolini needed some form of victorious military operation to push for an even more radical Fascist agenda at home. Probably no one but Mussolini knows. Like the overgrown schoolyard bully he was, Mussolini picked on a nation that couldn't possibly fight back. Italy conquered Ethiopia in a matter of days, practicing a "zero tolerance" policy, legitimizing attacks on civilians, and ultimately killing almost ten percent of Ethiopia's population. Mussolini also authorized the use of chemical warfare against civilians. This did not go unnoticed, and a number of important nations, including Britain and France, imposed economic sanctions on Italy.

(In an interesting side note, Mussolini's forces didn't manage to kill Ethiopian ruler Haile Selassie, who got away and would later become the Messianic figure of Rostafarianism, giving millions of stoners a quasi-religious justification for their recreational activities).

Mussolini claimed the sanctions were proof that other nations were trying to keep Italy down. He felt betrayed because, since he opposed Hitler, he expected Britian, France, and others to support him. But the sanctions were all Mussolini needed to drive him into Hitler's arms. The two signed a Rome-Berlin Axis agreement, in which Mussolini declared he had no problem with Germany annexing Austria—the chief stumbling block in German-Italian relations so far. Later, the two formed a full military alliance called the Pact of Steel.

Unfortunately, Mussolini's Ethiopian war had essentially bankrupted Italy. All the money earmarked for shoring up Italy's military was spent on the war. To cover costs, Mussolini was obliged to devalue Italy's currency. In the end, his pact with Hitler was essentially necessary because Germany, Britian and France were all involved in a desperate arms race, one Italy was woefully behind in. Kicking the crap out of Ethiopia was one thing—fighting a modernized European nation was another, and Mussolini wasn't getting in the ring without Hitler's assistance. The two are said by some sources to have disliked one another—they certainly didn't trust one another—but pragmatism made them bedfellows, and Hitler had quite a bit of respect for Mussolini, at first. Both nations spent a large amount of money sending men, materiel, and support to Fascist rebels in Spain. Another reason Mussolini threw in his lot with Hitler was his belief that nations where population was declining—that is, Britain and France—were "womanly," while nations with expanding populations were more virile, and through some twisted version of Darwinism, better. Mussolini himself quipped, "it's better to join the strong than join the weak."

But this wasn't entirely popular at home, with one prominent commentator saying Mussolini was "licking Hitler's boots." The Italian King (who was still around, if under Mussolini's thumb) preferred to remain neutral. He realized that with things as they were, the alliance during wartime would effectively mean putting Italy's foreign policy under Hitler's control. Even Mussolini, when he signed the Pact of Steel, knew Italy wasn't ready for a "real war," and signed on the understanding Germany wouldn't start a war for three more years. In the meantime, Mussolini sought an easy war, and conquered Albania in only five days.

When Germany annexed Poland and war was officially declared by the Allies, however, Mussolini chose to remain neutral, and even Hitler accepted this, knowing the three-year period had not yet passed. However, during the early stages of the war, when Germany looked more or less unstoppable, Mussolini wisely chose to go ahead and throw in whole-heartedly with the Nazis, and declared war against Britain and France.

Under Hitler's influence, Mussolini began persecuting Italian Jews, and sent many northward for Hitler to do as he would with—although, to be fair, Mussolini never subscribed to the concept of a "master race." He attempted to help Hitler and himself at the same time by attacking British forces in Africa, which met with some initial successes.

But Mussolini's success in war would not last. He invaded Greece, but didn't count on the Greeks fighting back as hard as they did, and ended up losing about a fourth of his gains in Albania, although later, with Hitler's help, the Axis would take the country. Furthermore, Mussolini's troops in Africa, after invading Egypt to fight the British, ran out of equipment and had to stop and wait to be resupplied. They were pushed back into Libya and fared so poorly against the British that Hitler was obliged to send troops to bail out his ally. These defeats in Greece and Africa, with Big Brother Hitler running to the rescue, grossly undermined Mussolini's support among the Italian people. This ill-feeling was exacerbated when Mussolini agreed to send troops to help Hitler invade the Soviet Union, which Italians didn't think was their fight. Worse, German troops had entered and occupied large parts of Italian territory to help defend it, and the Italian people, by and large, were deeply uncomfortable with it.

The telling blow came when America entered the war and invaded Sicily. People there hated their German "allies" so much that many welcomed the Allies as liberators. It was now quite clear to Mussolini that the Americans, led by General Dwight D. Eisenhower, would naturally see Sicily as an invasion point for the most vulnerable part of Axis Europe—the Italian peninsula. At this point Mussolini begged Hitler to sign a temporary peace with Stalin and to reassign German troops westward to help defend Italy. Hitler more or less ignored this plea. With Italian forces suffering so many defeats, Hitler called Mussolini to a conference to explain himself, which humiliated Mussolini, who wrote that he was tired of Hitler's "boasting." The very same day, the Allies bombed the city of Rome, which could not have improved Il Duce's mood.

Everything quickly went to hell in Italy after that. Key members of Mussolini's own party denounced him, and citizens had started regularly listening to Radio London to get news that wasn't censored and rewritten by the Fascist authorities. Mussolini summoned a conference of the Fascist leaders to try to garner support, but he was almost physically attacked when he told them Germany was thinking of withdrawing troops from southern Italy (which was in imminent danger of attack by America).

The council formalized a vote of "No Confidence" in Mussolini, and asked that the King be restored to full power. Despite this, Mussolini still showed up at his office the next day, and sought a meeting with the King. Before he could speak, the King cut him off and said he was being replaced by the more moderate Pietro Bagdolio, who, while on the surface keeping up appearances of alliance with the Axis, began secretly negotiating with Allied forces for Italy's surrender. When Italy signed a cease-fire with the Allies, Bagdolio and the King fled from Rome and left the army without orders. The nation was thrown into utter chaos, with conditions approaching a civil war. Mussolini himself was arrested, and Italy declared war on Germany. But the nation was still divided. The government fled to the Allied-controlled south, while German-supporting Italians retreated to strongholds in the north of Italy.

However, Mussolini was rescued by a band of German commandos, and placed in nominal charge of a new Italian state in the north. But everyone—especially Mussolini—knew he had become a mere puppet of the German military, and although he continued his bombastic speeches, he had absolutely no real power of his own. He spent his time helping Hitler execute the occasional Italian who'd pissed him off (including Mussolini's son-in-law), and writing his memoirs, entitled "My Rise and Fall." Mussolini fell into a pit of severe depression, although he seems at this late stage to have finally realized the reality of his situation. He gave an interview just a few months before his death, in which he famously said:

"Seven years ago, I was an interesting person. Now, I am little more than a corpse...I am finished. My star has fallen. I work and I try, yet know that all is but a farce...I await the end of the tragedy."

That end wasn't long in coming. With the defeat of Germany looming, and Allied-backed Italians inching ever closer, Mussolini and his mistress decided to flee to Spain. But Italian partisans recognized him, captured his party, and summarily shot Mussolini and his mistress. Their bodies were returned to Rome where the enraged citizens mutilated and hung up their bodies on meat-hooks in public. The morbidly curious among you will be pleased to know you can find gruesome photographs of this event all over the internet.

Mussolini's corpse was later salvaged by his supporters, and hidden away until after the war, when the dictator was at least granted a decent burial in a crypt with the symbols of his personal standard and an idealized portrait bust.

Today, Mussolini is largely regarded by historians as

the jackass he was. Clearly, his flip-flopping ideological, political and religious stances provided flimsy excuses for his natural violent tendencies.

Sadly, he's not the only world leader we can say that about.

Unpleasant Trivia...

• Believe it or not, there are some folks out there who won't drive a Volkswagen because it was supposedly Hitler's brain-child and the company used forced labor during World War II. But many Proud Americans are happy to drive a Ford. Turns out, Hitler loved Henry Ford. In fact, Der Fuhrer called Ford "my inspiration and my idol" and kept a framed photograph of Ford in his office. Turns out, Henry Ford advocated, in writing, the use of violence to exterminate the Jewish race. He blamed them for both Communism and those pesky labor unions that were cutting into his profits. He even wrote a book about his beliefs called "The International Jew." It was a best-seller in Germany, and the Nazi Party was so impressed with it they awarded Ford with the Grand Cross of the Eagle, the highest honor Nazi Germany could offer. It was one of Ford's proudest possessions. Even after the war, when the stories and photographic evidence of Nazi atrocities came to light, Ford famously refused to disown the Nazis or give up his precious Grand Cross of the Eagle. So next time you fire up that Ford truck, remember that.

• Franklin Delano Roosevelt is remembered as a great president who led us through the Great Depression and World War II. Not as well-known is his long affair with his wife Eleanor's secretary, Lucy Mercer. It started in 1918 and lasted for the rest of Roosevelt's life. There was a short break—at one point Eleanor discovered love letters and threatened to divorce Roosevelt, which in those days would have destroyed him, politically. He swore never to see Lucy again, and he and Eleanor slept in separate beds forever after. But he didn't keep his promise for long. One fact the U.S. government kept from the press was that, as Roosevelt lay on his deathbed, Eleanor was nowhere to be found. But right there by his side to the very end was Lucy Mercer.

A homeopath with a penchant for showgirls and homicide, he was a "gentle murderer"—and would have gotten away with it, too, if it wasn't for a pesky Scotland Yard inspector.

HAWLEY HARVEY CRIPPEN

Hawley Harvey Crippen was a doctor who married a wanna-be showgirl and regretted it. He preferred to live with his mistress while avoiding any social stigma. His solution? Murder.

The Crippen case is historically significant, because it provides an early example of chemical forensic evidence helping to convict a murderer, and it was the very first time wireless technology was used to aid in the capture of an international fugitive. But it wasn't chemicals or Marconi waves that did Crippen in—it was a few extremely poor, panick-stricken decisions that undermined an otherwise foolproof murder. He would have gotten away with it but for his own jackassery.

Crippen was born at the start of the American Civil War in Michigan, the son of a dry goods merchant who was prosperous enough to send his son to the Michigan School of Homeopathic Medicine. Crippen married Charlotte Bell, a lively young Irish-American girl, who bore him a son, Hawley Otto. But when the boy was two years old, Charlotte suddenly died of a stroke. Crippen asked his parents, who had retired to California, to raise the boy there. Meanwhile, Crippen moved to New York City, where he intended to start practice as a homeopath. Instead, he began working for Dr. Munyon's Homeopathic Remedies, a pharmaceutical company that developed and sold patent medicines. He also met the woman with whom his fate would be intertwined.

Cora Turner, aka "Bell Elmore," an aspiring music hall singer, was born Kunigunde Mackamotski to parents from Eastern Europe. She was a charming, free-spirited woman who was known to practice "free love" and openly have sexual affairs. Contemporaries said she was not above using her sexuality to advance her singing career. Crippen was obsessed with her beauty and liberated nature, and she with his medical degree and title. The two were soon married.

Dr. Munyon's transferred Crippen to Philadelphia, then across the Atlantic to London, England. Crippen lived off commissions on the sale of patent medicines, and he hoped to supplement his income by practicing homeopathy in London. He learned that his U.S. medical credentials weren't accepted in England, and he was barred from working as a doctor. Nevertheless, he and Cora lived in high style, and began to socialize with the great English variety players (singers and stage actors) of the day, including Kate Williams, aka Vulcana, who had a strongwoman act, and Lil Hawthorne of the Hawthorne Sisters. Both of them became close confidants of Cora's.

Crippen was devoted to his wife's singing career, and he spent so much time trying to launch and manage it that Dr. Munyon's Homeopathic Remedies fired him. He managed to get a job as the manager for Drouet's Institution for the Deaf, where, just after the dawn of the 20th century, he met a young typist named Ethel Le Neve. She was conservative and educated—quite the opposite of Cora. Crippen became infatuated with her. Meanwhile, Crippen's diminished salary was not providing the lifestyle Cora wanted, so she insisted they take on lodgers in their Camden Road house in London in order to gain extra income.

One day, however, Crippen came home to catch Cora *in flagrante delicto* with one of those boarders. Seeing no further need for marital fidelity, he openly took Le Neve as his mistress. Crippen and Cora argued constantly, each berating the other for their change in fortunes, the failure of Cora's singing career, and the unraveling marriage. At one point Cora threatened to publicly expose her own and Crippen's infidelities—that is, to commit a sort of social suicide, and take Crippen's reputation with her. At this point Crippen reportedly told friends he was deeply concerned about Cora's physical and mental health.

For two years this untenable situation lingered on, until one night when the Crippens hosted a party in their home. Cora's friends never saw her again after that night—she'd completely disappeared. Crippens told friends who called to see her, including Kate Williams and Lil Hawthorne, that Cora had left suddenly for the United States, to visit an ailing relative. A few weeks later, he told them Cora herself had sickened and died in California, and been cremated there.

Meanwhile, Cora's friends thought it distasteful and suspicious that Le Neve had moved into Crippen's house within a few weeks of the disappearance, and was openly wearing Cora's jewelry and fine clothes. Kate Williams reported her suspicions to the police, but they did not take "Vulcana" the strongwoman seriously. However, Cora's other confidant was more well-connected. The head of Scotland Yard received a request from a friend for a personal favor—to investigate Cora's disappearance. The friend was John Nash, husband of Lil Hawthorne.

Chief Inspector Walter Dew of Scotland Yard was put on the case. He dutifully searched Crippen's house, but found nothing incriminating. He was convinced, however, that Crippen was lying to him in the initial phases of their interview, so kept pressing. Crippen admitted that he had invented the story about Cora dying in California. He did it, he said, to save himself from personal embarrassment. He claimed Cora had fled for Chicago with Bruce Williams, a London stage actor. Dew was satisfied with the explanation, and recommended to his superiors that the investigation be closed.

This is where "the jackass factor" enters our tale—Dew, like any good investigator, played his cards close to his vest. While he didn't suspect Crippen of wrongdoing, Crippen didn't know that. The night of the interview, a panic-stricken Crippen and Le Neve fled to the Netherlands, and the next day they boarded a trans-Atlantic steamer, the Montrose, bound for Canada.

Word of Crippen's flight soon reached Dew, who realized he'd been mistaken. He ordered another three searches of the house, each one more thorough. He became frustrated, but on the final search, his efforts paid off. Dew's team found, buried under the basement bricks, half of a human corpse with a distinctive scar on its abdomen. They also found part of a specific type of male pajama top with bleached-blonde hairs on it, and, elsewhere in the home, traces of the "downer" drug scopolamine. When the remains were tested chemically, Scotland Yard found they contained the toxic compound then known as hyoscine.

Meanwhile, Crippen and Le Neve were still

somewhere in the mid-Atlantic. Never one to stint at spending, Crippen was sure to travel first-class. He tried to disguise himself by shaving his mustache and starting to grow out his beard. Le Neve traveled dressed as a boy. Traveling first class puts one in contact with the more important members of the crew, and the captain of the steamer was accustomed to circulating among the high-class passengers. He realized Le Neve wasn't a boy, and began to put two and two together, since he'd heard wireless telegram reports about the fugitives. Just a few nautical miles before the Montrose would have been out of transmitter range, he sent a wireless telegraph to Scotland Yard, describing the couple and sharing his suspicions. Again, the jackass factor—had Crippen been able to bring himself to travel third class, he would have been extremely unlikely to ever run into the captain personally.

Dew, receiving this, quickly booked passage on a much faster ocean liner, the Laurentic, and charged on to Quebec in Canada, arriving some time before Crippen on the Montrose. When the Montrose entered the St. Lawrence River, Dew came on board disguised as one of the local pilots who would guide the ship into port. The captain, playing his part to perfection, asked Crippen and Le Neve if they'd like the honor of meeting the pilots. When he was introduced to Crippen, Dew took off his disguise and said, "Do you know me?" Crippen, after a long pause, bowed his head, sighed deeply, and said: "Thank God it's over. The suspense has been too great. I couldn't stand it any longer." He and Le Neve were promptly arrested and returned to England. Again, the jackass factor: as an American citizen, had Crippen sailed to the United States, Dew would have had a long, complex extradition battle ahead of him.

Since Crippen was caught in Canada, then a dominion of the British Empire, he was easily sent back to London to face justice.

Both went on trial separately in October, 1910. Crippen's defense said the remains found in the house were much older than 1905, when Crippen and Cora had moved in—thus Crippen could not be the killer, and the body was not Cora's. Crippen stuck to his story about Cora running away to Chicago with a lover.

But the prosecution pointed out that the scar on the abdomen was consistent with Cora's medical history. They also showed that the male pajama tops with traces of bleached-blonde hair were manufactured no earlier than 1908, proving that the body had been buried during Crippen's tenure at the house.

It took the jury only 27 minutes to declare Crippen guilty. He was hanged the following month. Le Neve, meanwhile, was tried as an accessory after the fact, but was acquitted. On the morning of Crippen's execution, she emigrated to America, asking that her photograph be placed in Crippen's coffin.

Today, various conspiracy theories abound, indicating that Crippen was innocent—of Cora's premeditated murder, at least. Some say he may have accidentally overdosed her with sedatives, then panicked. Others speculate he was conducting illegal abortions on the property, something went wrong, a patient died, and he panicked and hid the evidence. Others wonder why he would bury only the torso and hide the rest of the body elsewhere. In 2007 some researchers tested the remains and said the body was not related to Cora's living relatives, and was in fact the body of a man, but the team's methodology, using "new techniques" only known to the research team, is in doubt by the medical and law enforcement communities, who have determined that the relatives may not be related to Cora by blood, only marriage. Scotland Yard has officially denied several requests from Crippen's living relatives for a posthumous pardon.

So if you've ever wondered how to go from homeopathy to homicide in one easy step, just consider the example of Crippen, a true Jackass of History.

Unpleasant Trivia...

• The Roman emperor Claudius was married four times. The first wife, Plautia, he divorced for adultery. Not only that, she was implicated in the murder of her stepsister. His second wife, Aelia Paetina, was a political liability, but she also subjected the stuttering, limping emperor to a barrage of emotional and mental abuse. Claudius's third marriage was to his cousin, Valeria Messalina. The fact that she was part of Caligula's inner circle should have been a red flag. Ancient historians are unanimous in saying Valeria was a nymphomaniac. She once donned a blonde wig and had a competition with a well-known prostitute to see who could have the most partners in one night. Valeria also manipulated Claudian policies to make herself filthy rich. Possessed of catastrophically bad judgment, she married her lover Gaius Silius in a public ceremony while Claudius was out of town. The two attempted a coup d'etat but were captured and executed. Claudius, apparently in all seriousness, ordered the Praetorian Guard to assassinate him if he ever tried to get married again. Ultimately he bowed to pressure, considered re-marrying his second wife, but eventually decided on the well-connected Agrippina. Claudius thought it would be a nice idea to adopt her son - a fellow named Nero. Eventually Agrippina poisoned Claudius and young Nero became the emperor of Rome, with disastrous results.

• During the American Civil War, General Joseph Hooker became well-known for losing spectacularly to Robert E. Lee at the Battle of Chancellorsville. He was also infamous for his considerable baggage train of prostitutes...which is why today we call them "hookers."

You know why African warlords chop off little kids' hands? They learned it from this guy. A selfish tyrant and borderline pedophile, he was, as one writer said, "wickedness triumphant."

KING LEOPOLD II

Leopold II was the king of Belgium from 1855 to 1909. He built lavishly, constructing many beautiful gardens and public buildings. In fact, some in Belgium call him "The Builder King" to this day. But most of us know him as "The Butcher of the Congo." Leopold managed to found a personal colony in Africa, exploited the Congo in a ruthless and needlessly cruel manner, and tried to cover up the evidence. He set the stage for horrors and atrocities in the Congo that continue still. That alone would make him a Jackass of History. The fact that he was also a borderline pedophile is just icing on the cake of jackassery.

Leopold wasn't destined to be king—he was the second son of the family, but his elder brother died before he was born. His mother was a French princess, and he was related on his father's side through German relatives to Queen Victoria of England. When he married Marie Henriette of Austria, the granddaughter of the so-called Holy Roman Emperor—a political arrangement—the marriage went unconsummated. It is said during a state visit to England, Queen Victoria and her husband, Prince Albert, had to explain the facts of life to the young couple. One wonders whether this was necessary—surely the two knew what they weren't doing. Nevertheless, the couple had four children, though Leopold's only son died of pneumonia after falling in a pond. His daughters were all married to foreign princes—political arrangements that would eventually get them ousted from their father's will.

Leopold's wife Marie Henriette was beautiful, charming and popular in the eyes of the Belgian people, who called her "The Rose." She was responsible for many benevolent acts toward the poor, and was known for her excellent horsemanship, insisting on caring for her horses herself. This led to popular jokes about the marriage of the "stableboy and the nun," with Leopold being the nun. He had a reputation for being shy and withdrawn, despite his smooth political patter. As it turns out, Leopold was no nun. Later in his reign (1885), sworn testimony in a British courtroom implicated Leopold in a human trafficking ring. It seems a British slaver received a regular salary to procure virgins for Leopold's bed. Most of these were kidnapped from London's notorious East End, and some were as young as 10. The British swept the case under the rug because it also implicated several Englishmen of high social and political standing. Perhaps because of his predilection for little girls, Leopold's marriage suffered. He and Marie Henriette lived separate lives, she retiring to live in the resort town of Spa until she died in 1902.

Leopold's father made him a member of the Belgian parliament as soon as he was old enough. Like Great Britain and many other monarchies by this time, the parliament and cabinet held most of the actual power, but the monarchy was retained for reasons of prestige. Nevertheless, Leopold was expected to play an important role in government and this time in parliament was to serve as his training period. Instead of applying himself, Leopold—only about 20 years old—

began to expound publicly his philosophy that Belgium was too small and weak, and that only an overseas colony would allow her to play a role in European affairs. He spent the next decade traveling extensively, visiting Egypt, much of the Mediterranean coast, India, China, and sub-Saharan Africa. When his father died, Leopold was made king at age 30.

As the King of Belgium, he did some good—or at least allowed some good to be done. The nation was in the midst of a bitter political war between the Liberal Party and the Catholic Party. The liberals managed to push through a law establishing free secular schools and ending public funding for Catholic education. The parliament also passed, without interference from Leopold, laws protecting workers, limiting the exploitation of children and women, allowing the formation of labor unions, and ensuring that workers got Sunday off.

But in the end, what Leopold focused on and cared about most was money. To get it, he'd make a mockery of all the workers' rights legislation passed in Belgium, none of which applied, in Leopold's mind, to sub-human Africans.

Leopold wanted the Philippines, and tried to persuade Spain to cede them to Belgium. This plan failed, as did a plan to establish an "independent" Philippines with a Belgian ruler. After several other failed attempts to get a state colony going, Leopold realized there was another way: what if he *personally* founded a colony? Perhaps to get him off their back about it, parliament actually lent Leopold some money to get things going. He promptly hired the famous African explorer Henry Stanley (of "Dr. Livingstone, I presume?" fame), to explore and claim lands in the Congo. Stanley spent five years on the extensive waterways of the Congo river basin, building roads, setting up forts and trading posts, and compelling native chiefs and kings to sign treaties of friendship with Leopold—not, it's important to realize, with Belgium, but with Leopold personally. These were mostly altered after-the-fact to indicate the chiefs ceded their entire lands to Leopold. It is doubtful many of the native rulers knew what they were signing, and several missionaries in the region began to complain about Stanley's brutal treatment of the natives and use of forced labor (Stanley, incidentally, holds the record of "most Africans murdered by an explorer").

European powers were always wrangling over territory in the delicate "balance of power" that worked about well enough to set the stage for two world wars. But at the Berlin Conference, Leopold managed to get the European powers and the United States to recognize his claim as the personal ruler of the Congo—an area about 75 times the size of Belgium itself. This sort of personal empire was essentially unique in modern history. Leopold, ever the spinner of negative press, cannily disguised his holding company as a philanthropic and scientific organization: "The International Association for the Exploration and Civilization of the Congo." So, by 1885, Leopold was the absolute ruler of the so-called "Congo Free State."

The first step was the formation of the Force Publique—a 19,000 strong private army of European mercenaries and ex-convicts. Their initial job was to extract as much ivory as possible from the Congo, but ivory didn't turn out to be as lucrative as Leopold had hoped. Luckily for him, and unluckily for the people of the Congo, the invention of the inflatable tire and a host of other new technologies created a world-wide rush for rubber. The Congo was an ideal climate for rubber plantations, but the plant takes an amazingly long time to cultivate. Wild rubber, however, was all over the rain forest in the form of the landolphia vine.

Mad for rubber, Leopold directed the Force Publique to exploit it in the most ruthless manner possible. Standard operating procedure was the the Force would march into a village, hold all the women and children hostage, and force the men to disperse into the rain forests to harvest a certain quota of wild rubber. If the quota wasn't met, the women and children wouldn't eat. If the harvested amount was especially low, the Force would cut off the hands of one of the man's children to motivate him to work harder. Furthermore, Leopold, who was financing all of this on his own, ordered that any Force soldier who shot a native had to show his superior officer the native's severed hand as proof of death—this was supposedly to ensure they didn't waste bullets or save them for a mutiny. When soldiers missed, they had no qualms about simply finding a living native and lopping off his or her hand to present to the officers. This happened all over the Congo, and it was documented by many missionaries and the British journalist E.D. Morel, who began to write about these atrocities, which stirred up outrage in the press, particularly in Britain, France, and America. However, Leopold was a master of controlling the press back home. He successfully bribed newspaper publishers to keep news of the atrocities out of the papers. He used his political power to silence the voices of protests among the highly politicized Belgian Catholics, and was fairly successful—at home, at least—of portraying anyone who spoke or wrote about the abuses as members of a vast Protestant conspiracy aimed and discrediting

Catholicism and advancing the colonial empires of other nations at the expense of Belgium. Nevertheless, the writer Algis Valiunas said Leopold's rule of the Congo was "wickedness triumphant...Leopold merits a place among the great modern enemies of civilization."

Meanwhile, things got worse, despite three statues that had been erected portraying Leopold as the savior of the Congolese. To facilitate the growing rubber trade, Leopold ordered forced native labor to build roads and chop wood for steam engine boilers. This, in addition to the forced rubber harvests, meant most men were unable to practice their traditional lifestyles of hunting, fishing and farming. A terrible famine descended on the Congo, along with outbreaks of smallpox and the "sweating sickness" that the Force Publique did nothing to alleviate. In fact, Leopold ordered almost all missionaries out of the country, which took away the one hope for proper health care the natives had. He allowed in a few missionaries, only on his personal sufferance and approved personally by him. He also closed the Congo to foreign business interests, although, as public criticism increased, Leopold offered substantial licenses to do business in the Congo to powerful American families like the Rockefellers and Guggenheims. This did little to prevent mounting calls for action.

Popular voices of the time got in on the public shaming of Leopold. Mark Twain wrote a satire in which Leopold praises himself for bringing Christianity to the Congo, saying a few deaths by murder and starvation were worth it. Booker T. Washington made several public speeches against the atrocities and lobbied for American intervention (which didn't happen). Arthur Conan Doyle, creator of Sherlock Holmes, wrote scathing articles calling Leopold to account for being "more concerned with how much he can extract...rather than making any attempt to uplift them (the Congolese) or modernize their condition."

By now, various sources estimated that, from a combination of murder, forced labor, famine, and rampant disease, that nearly half the population of the Congo had died under Leopold's rule. Hundreds of thousands of refugees fled into neighboring territories with horror stories. Others fled into the rainforests to eke out a living as best they could. The terrible conditions also exacerbated ethnic tensions, and the open animosity between the Tutsi and Hutu people dates from this period. It also doesn't take much of a stretch to connect the African warlords' penchant for mutilation to practices learned from the Force Publique.

Unfortunately, several other colonial powers also practiced forced labor and were guilty of atrocities of their own. But in the political climate of the day, it was much easier to direct anger and outrage against Leopold, because he was the sole ruler of the Congo as a private citizen—it was not a Belgian colony, just Leopold's.

Leopold did use his wealth in one productive way— he built a slew of important civic buildings in Belgium, expanding the royal palace, creating a lovely botanical garden for the public, and other noteworthy structures that still stand. He also built lavish private buildings for himself and his underage mistresses, including a magnificent palace on the French Riviera, where he spent most of his time. While the public gladly accepted his civic building program, they were increasingly disgusted with his denigration in the media of Belgium's small size and influence, of his not-so-hidden interest in underage girls, and, as Leopold's bribery and intimidation of the media grew less effective, revelations about the horrors he ordered in the Congo.

In his declining years, a major blow to Leopold's popularity was his public relationship with his mistress—which was normal enough for a king. But Belgium's mostly conservative population was not happy about the 65-year-old king's latest mistress—a 16-year-old prostitute named Caroline Lacroix, who he lavished with wealth and meaningless noble titles (and with whom he had two sons). This relationship became the target of many satirical cartoons and editorials in the press and was seen as something of a public embarrassment for the entire nation.

Ultimately, the Belgian parliament had enough. In a legal action, they forced Leopold to cede his entire dominion in the Congo to the nation of Belgium, which would take it on as an official state colony. He was either too tired to fight it, or already had amassed so much wealth he didn't care any more. He retired to his Riviera home with his teenage mistress, where he died a year later. He was so unpopular that when his funeral procession passed through Belgium, it was actually booed by the populace. Needless to say, the statue of himself he'd erected in Kinshasa, a city in the Congo, was pulled down immediately. But two other statues in Blankenberge and Ostend, back home, show him as a savior of the Congolese. In 2004, an acivist cut off the Ostend statue's hand as a reminder of the hands lopped off by Leopold's private army. The city council decided not to replace the hand, but leave it as-is. In 2005, the Congo's culture minister ordered that the Kinshasa statue be replaced—after all, he said, Leopold should be recognized for the good he did, as well as the bad. But within hours of the statue's re-erection, the same official ordered it taken back down, after thousands of Congolese threatened to riot.

Some historians take a moderate view of Leopold, seeing him as no worse than any other colonial potentate of the time. Others say he can't be blamed for the actions of the Force Publique—after all, Leopold never personally set foot in Belgium. The real question is whether Leopold knew what was going on. I think the evidence suggests he did—early on, he took pains to disguise his true aims in the Congo as philanthropic. He was bothered enough to attempt to censor or discredit anyone who reported the atrocities that happened on his watch.

Finally, the proof that he was personally responsible, in my opinion, is that just before his death, he ordered that all of his files related to the Congo be burned. He'd never turned over any of those documents to the state of Belgium, despite repeated requests. Every record was completely destroyed, leaving what Leopold knew about and what he didn't to the realm of eternal speculation. But you don't destroy records that would exonerate you. He was so estranged from his daughters that, not wanting them or their foreign husbands to inherit any of his wealth or property, left all his personal buildings to the State of Belgium, where they are still used today for public business. He also left his wealth to his teenage mistress, which prompted a vicious legal battle between her, the state, and Leopold's daughters that was never quite resolved to anyone's satisfaction.

To his last breath, Leopold insisted he was responsible for leading the Congolese out of savagery and converting them to Christianity. In the end, however, the world has judged Leopold II of Belgium, and found him guilty of being a Jackass of History.

"Single white female seeks affluent gentleman to join economic fortunes. Must enjoy being chloroformed, chopped up, and buried in a hog pen. Serious inquiries only."

BELLE GUNNESS

What makes a jackass? The definition is unclear. Most of us would think of a jackass as foolish or stupid. I like to extend that to include the incompetent, the arrogant, the mean, and the just plain evil. Whatever Belle Gunness was, she certainly wasn't foolish or stupid. She ranks among the Jackasses of History, but she was one of the smartest and most successful—and most evil—jackasses we've yet met. At first alone, and later with the help of a demented henchman, Ray Lamphere (himself an utter jackass), she killed at least a dozen people, including two husbands, five of her own children, and a long list of would-be suitors. She is suspected of killing at least 40 people. But her fate remains a mystery, and the headless woman buried in her grave is probably not her.

Belle was born in Norway in 1859 to a stonemason. She was the youngest of eight children. A legend about her early adulthood might shed some light on her later actions: in 1877, she went to a dance while pregnant. A local rich boy who was too deep in his cups had a physical altercation with her and kicked her in the stomach. She miscarried. But the boy was rich and well-connected, and Norwegian authorities declined to prosecute him. Belle's friends and family said her personality radically changed from that time forward.

The assailant died a year later from "stomach cancer," but an autopsy wasn't done and his symptoms were also consistent with strychnine poisoning.

Belle resolved to leave Norway entirely after this, and, working on a farm for three years, saved enough money for a steamship to America. She next surfaces in Chicago, where in 1884 she married fellow Norwegian Mads Sorenson. Together, they opened a confectioner's shop. It was disastrously unsuccessful, and in less than a year, the store mysteriously burned down. The couple collected on their fire insurance policy and bought a fine house in Chicago.

Sorenson and Belle had four children (some authorities disagree). Two of them died in infancy of "acute colitis," the symptoms of which were almost indistinguishable (at the time) from multiple forms of poisoning. Both of the infants had life insurance, and Belle collected on both deaths. Then Sorenson himself died in the summer of 1900—July 30, to be exact, which is the one day that two life insurance policies Belle had taken out on him just happened to overlap. She received the equivalent of about $240,000 in today's money. One doctor said Sorenson died of strychnine poisoning. Belle insisted on a second opinion, and another doctor said it was heart failure. An autopsy was never performed, despite the suspicions of Sorenson's family, who launched an unsuccessful campaign to have the body exhumed to search for traces of strychnine or arsenic. By then, authorities had cleared Belle of any wrongdoing and chalked the death up to natural causes.

She used the proceeds to buy another fine house in Chicago, and also, more importantly, a farm in La Porte, Indiana. As she was preparing to move to La Porte, the boat house and carriage house of her second Chicago home burned down, and she collected a substantial insurance payment. Also as she was preparing to move, Belle met another Norwegian-born widower with two daughters, Peter Gunness, and married him. A week after the wedding, his infant daughter died while left alone in Belle's care. Months later, Peter also died in what we can only call a "bizarre kitchen accident." Belle told police Peter had been leaning over the stove to reach a pair of slippers, fell and was scalded with brine while simultaneously, part of a sausage-making machine fell off a high shelf and hit him in the head. Local folk were incredulous—Peter was a respected butcher and wasn't known to be so clumsy. His brother came and took the second daughter to Wisconsin—this little girl would be the only child to have survived living with Belle.

Belle collected the modern equivalent of about $86,000 from Peter's life insurance policy. Enough local people didn't believe her story, and the county coroner in fact ruled that Peter had been murdered. However, Belle managed to convince the district attorney that she had nothing to do with it. She was not charged and the ruling of "murder" was essentially ignored by the sheriff's office. About this time, Belle had a baby—she would have had to have been pregnant prior to meeting Peter.

Belle continued to work the farm with the help of a hired hand, Ray Lamphere. After a few years, her foster daughter, Jennie Olson, who'd lived with her since her first marriage, disappeared. She told people Jennie had gone away to finishing school in California.

About this time, Belle placed advertisements in all of the Chicago papers and most major Midwest dailies saying she was a "comely widow" with a productive farm, and she was seeking "a gentleman equally well provided" to "join fortunes."

Over the next few years a steady stream of would-be suitors showed up in La Porte to court Belle and, with one exception, were never heard from again. Just a few examples:

Jon Moe from Minnesota showed up with $1,000 to pay off Belle's mortgage. He disappeared a week later. Ole Budsberg, an elderly widower from Wisconsin, was last seen cashing out his mortgage on his Wisconsin property at a bank in La Porte. He withdrew several thousand dollars in cash and was never seen again. When his sons wrote Belle to ask after his health, she told him he had never arrived in La Porte to her knowledge. Andrew Helgelien of South Dakota exchanged letters with Belle, who declared her love for him after a brief period of correspondence. He took out his entire life savings and went to La Porte. Andrew and Belle were seen together at the bank in La Porte, depositing his savings into her account. That was the last time anyone saw him. She deposited large sums of cash by herself twice in the following weeks.

Those were just a few of a large number of men who disappeared after going to see Belle. Only one man lived to tell the tale, and it was a strange one. George Anderson of Tarkio, Missouri, came to La Porte to meet Belle. They agreed that if they got married, George would pay off her mortgage and provide some other funds she said she needed. He later reported waking that night in the guest bedroom to find Belle standing over him with "a guttering candle and a sinister look on her face." The incident freaked Anderson out so badly he fled the house and took the first train back to Missouri.

In a move that would only later seem suspicious, Belle

began having huge trunks delivered to her farm. The delivery driver said he was amazed at her strength, as she would heft up onto her shoulders trunks he could barely lift. Neighbors thought it odd that Belle kept the shutters to her house closed day and night. Occasionally, farmers and passersby would notice her digging late at night in the hog pen. All of this, of course, was only weird in retrospect.

In the meantime, however, things were getting out of hand between Belle and her hired hand, Ray Lamphere. Lamphere was in love with Belle and did whatever she asked. Although utterly devoted to her, he became jealous at the constant stream of would-be suitors. He began to "make scenes" and Belle fired him. She immediately appeared at the local courthouse, saying Lamphere was insane. She convinced a judge to convene a sanity hearing, but Lamphere passed with flying colors. After he was declared sane, Belle said she'd seen him stalking around the farm late at night, and that she felt threatened by him. He was arrested for trespassing, but the charge wasn't particularly serious and he was let go.

During this, Asle Helgelien, the brother of would-be suitor Andrew, started writing to Belle asking after his brother. She told him Andrew had decided to return to Norway. Asle didn't believe that for one minute, but Belle brazenly offered to coordinate a local search for Andrew. However, she warned, such a search would be very expensive and Asle would have to send her some money to pay for it. He said he'd come to La Porte and they'd talk further.

With Asle on the way, and Lamphere as a dangerous wild card, Belle needed to take quick action. She visited a La Porte lawyer and told her that Lamphere had come to her house, argued with her, and threatened to kill her and her children and burn down their house for good measure. She went so far as to write a will, saying she was certain Lamphere would kill her. Within a few days she went to the bank and paid off all the outstanding debt on her property. Oddly—or not so oddly—she did not report any of Lamphere's threats to the sheriff. In retrospect, it seems clear she was setting him up for an arson charge at the very least.

Weeks later, a young man named Joe Maxson—who Belle had hired to replace Lamphere—woke in the middle of the night, too warm to sleep. He noticed smoke coming in under the door of the spare bedroom where he slept—opening it, he saw the outer hall was a wall of flame. Maxson managed to leap from the second-floor window and run to town for help. By the time the old-school hook-and-ladder from the fire brigade got there, however, the farmhouse was reduced to a pile of smoking rubble.

Inside, investigators found the bodies of Belle's children in their beds, along with the headless corpse of a woman. Authorities played the part Belle had set for them and immediately arrested Lamphere, charging him with murder and arson. Not only did Belle's lawyer implicate him, but a neighbor boy said he saw Lamphere running away from the farmhouse.

Meanwhile everyone agreed that the headless woman probably wasn't Belle—after all, the corpse appeared to be about 5'3" and Belle was almost six feet tall. The shoe size of the corpse didn't match the size of shoes Belle ordered at the local store. The county coroner sent the stomach contents of the corpse to Chicago for testing, and they came back positive for strychnine. A local miner was hired to sift through the wreckage for teeth, at the suggestion of Belle's dentist. While no one ever found the head, they conveniently found a set of Belle's false teeth. The coroner—either weak-willed, lazy, or negligent—agreed that the body must be Belle's, since her teeth were found nearby.

But Asle Helgelien had arrived in La Porte, and he was adamant that his brother Andrew had been a victim of foul play. He wouldn't let up, but the sheriff wasn't willing to do much until handyman Joe Maxson came forward with a story no one could ignore. He said Belle ordered him to haul wheelbarrows full of dirt to the farm's hog pen, where there were many depressions in the ground. Belle said they were covered rubbish pits, and asked Maxson to use the dirt to level off the ground. The sheriff took 12 men back to the site and started to dig—and that's when it became evident to almost everyone that Belle was a murderess.

The first body they found was that of Jennie Olson, Belle's foster daughter who had supposedly gone off to finishing school. Then they found the unidentified bodies of two small children. Then, to Asle's horror, they found the body of Andrew Helgelien...then Ole Budsberg...then Jon Moe...and so on. Overall, more than a dozen bodies were found, but the work of burial and exhumation was crudely done, so authorities couldn't pin down an exact number of corpses.

When Lamphere went to trial, he was acquitted of murder, especially after Maxson testified that he'd seen the miner who sifted the wreckage plant Belle's false teeth. But the jury did find Lamphere guilty of arson, and he was sentenced to 20 years in prison. He soon died of tuberculosis. But on his deathbed, he confessed all to the Reverend E.A. Schell: that Belle had killed some 40 people, and that he'd helped her kill a few and buried some of the bodies. He said she planned the fire, chloroformed her children, and hired a housekeeper from out-of-town, who she promptly murdered and beheaded, throwing her head into a swamp (it was never recovered). Then she torched the house and fled to a prearranged rendezvous with Lamphere. He was to put her on a train to Chicago. But she never showed up at their meeting. She betrayed and framed him.

Bankers verified that most of her savings—about $6.3 million in today's money, all ill-gotten—had been withdrawn from the bank in the days before the fire.

But no one ever found Belle Gunness—at least, not beyond the shadow of a doubt.

For many years after, "Gunness sightings" were reported in Chicago, New York, Los Angeles, and San Fransisco, just to name a few. The La Porte sheriff received about two reports a month until the early 1930s.

In 1931, an elderly woman of Norwegian descent calling herself "Esther Carlson" was arrested in Los Angeles for the poisoning death of a local businessman who had added her name to his bank accounts in the weeks before his demise. The death was initially ruled a heart attack, but the victim's son discovered discrepancies in his father's financial records. Detectives put two and two together and arrested Carlson and another woman.

It is not known who first made the connection between Esther Carlson and Belle Gunness, but California detectives had witnesses from La Porte look at Carlson's photo. At least two swore they believed it was a much thinner, older Belle. Further damning evidence—that, to my mind, clinches it—was found when detectives discovered in Carlson's home several bottles of poison along with framed photos of Belle's children.

However, Carlson escaped justice for the LA murder by dying in jail before the trial. If Carlson was Belle, she managed to escape justice for all of her crimes, too. In 2007 authorities used DNA from the farmhouse remains, an envelope Belle had licked, and the living descendants of Belle's sisters in the hope of solving the mystery once and for all, but there was not enough usable DNA to make a conclusive analysis.

So for now, the fate of Belle Gunness remains a mystery, although I don't know why anyone would keep photos of the dead children of a serial killer. I think Carlson was Belle. But we'll never know. All we do know is that Belle's brazenness and cold-blooded actions maker her a jackass on the evil side, while frankly, Ray Lamphere is a class-A Jackass of History on the incompetent side. Either way, both are Jackasses of History.

Unpleasant Trivia...

• Sergius III was Pope from 897 to 911, and is considered one of the worst. His pontificate began with the military backing of a powerful noble family who were irritated with the previous pope and were determined to install a friendly one. Sergius III is the only pope (that we know of!) to order the murder of other popes (his predecessors Leo V and Christopher) and to have fathered an illegitimate child who also became pope (John XI). He gave unprecedented power to a notorious courtesan, Theodora, who papal historian Liutprand called a "shameless whore" and who wielded so much power another historian called Sergius's reign a "pornocracy." Sergius took up with her daughter, Marozia, with whom he lived openly as his mistress. He fathered a child by her who would grow up to become Pope John XI—he wasn't a bad guy, but was utterly dominated by his mother and brother, who secretly ruled the Church.

When you're handsome and speak well, you can start wars for fun, flout convention, and seduce queens. But you'll still wake up with your house on fire and an agry mob outside.

ALCIBIADES THE ATHENIAN

This time let's travel to ancient Greece and meet one of my favorite jackasses of history—Alcibiades. I almost admire him sometimes—there was a lot to admire about him—but in the end, it's clear he was a jackass of the worst sort, because although he was utterly self-serving, as many people loved as hated him.

Alcibiades is one of the most successful jackasses in history, though he came to a bad end. In all the surviving ancient Greek writing, the person most castigated and defamed is Alcibiades, and yet he also had all the makings of a great hero. He was a manipulator, a side-switcher, a spy, a traitor, a general, a rabble-rousing orator, and yet his personal charisma was so great that he was able to repeatedly talk his way out of his crimes, often being lauded and applauded by the very people he screwed over in the first place.

Alcibiades was, in fact, the most important cause of the decline of Athens from its classical brilliance to being reduced to a Spartan-dominated wasteland. Athens diminished after that, and never achieved its former glory—all due to the ambition and massive ego of one man. But his good qualities, his able leadership as a general and statesman, his great beauty and powerful personality ensured he delayed his comeuppance until it was too late to save the society he is chiefly responsible for destroying.

His shifting sides in the Peloponnesian War earned him a reputation for cunning and treachery. He was good-looking and rich, affected a (for the time) distinguished lisp, and was as well known for his extravagant lifestyle and loose morals as for his eloquent, if self-serving, statesmanship.

Alcibiades was born in 450 BCE in Athens, the son of a powerful politician, Cleinias, who had died in battle but who was supposedly a descent of the Odysseus of Greek myth. Alcibiades' mother, Deinomache, was from the powerful aristocratic family Alkmeonidai, which also spawned Pericles, generally regarded as the most able statesman of Athenian history. In fact, Pericles was Alcibiades' uncle and legal guardian.

Some anecdotes from the time indicate the nature of Alcibiades' jackassery. First of all, Plutarch says that of all his character flaws, the worst one was his ruthless ambition and desire for superiority over others. This seems clear from his youth. Yet he was a master of turning negatives into positives. For example, he hated to lose so badly, that, when set to wrestle another student, he bit the student's hand. "Alcidiades," said the loser, "bites like a woman!" Alcibiades responded, "No, like a lion!" Alcibiades is also said to have murdered one of his own servants by beating him with a staff. He was so beautiful that every dirty old man in Athens was after him. One story goes that a fellow called Anytus was obsessed with him and begged for his favors. He invited Alcibiades to a party, but Alcibiades refused the invitation. Getting very drunk at home, he changed his mind, showed up to the party, and without speaking a word, carried off half the gold and silver plates and cups. Anytus was so besotted with him that he told guests Alcibiades had shown great restraint by not taking all of it. As a young man, he publicly gave a box on the ear to a noble old man, Hipponicus, for no other reason that that his friends dared him to. The entire community was outraged, but Alcibiades went to Hipponicus' house, presented himself naked, and told the old man to do what he pleased with him. Hipponicus supposedly forgot his resentment and immediately offered Alcibiades his daughter in marriage. Later, she (called Hipparete) was offended by her husband's constant affairs and went to the equivalent of a divorce court. Alcibiades showed up, physically picked her up and carried her back home. No one tried to stop him. She was shut away in his house and died not long after.

And repeatedly, the authorities and the public let him get away with this sort of behavior, even after his famous uncle was dead. Alcibiades had that much charisma.

Alcibiades was also a student and favorite of the philosopher Socrates, with whom he had a sexual relationship as well as a profound personal respect. Socrates was attracted to Alcadiades' beauty and potential; Alcibiades was attracted to Socrates' intellect, and, early on, virtuous nature. They defended one another on the battlefield on two recorded occasions. But the two later had a falling-out, as Alcibiades became the sort of politician that Socrates despised.

To truly appreciate Alcibiades, you have to consider the context of his time: Greece was wracked by a war between Athens and Sparta, and their attendant allies. All you really need to know about the Peloponnesian War was that it was a decades-long clusterfuck of history, as the jealous and ambitious Greeks, fresh from defeating the mighty Persian Empire, decided to viciously squabble amongst themselves and lay waste one another's cities and farmland for the next 30 years. Thucydides' famous history of the war makes it clear the entire thing was a lamentable, preventable tragedy and waste of time and resources, throwing Greece into a turmoil that allowed Alexander the Great's father to waltz in and own the place a generation later.

Alcibiades was a major player in this terrible war—further, he essentially re-started it after a peace treaty had been signed. He switched sides so many times, it's a wonder anyone ever trusted him. But he had a pretty face and a golden tongue, and was a master of manipulation. Lesser men—and bigger jackasses—have risen to even loftier heights.

When he was 30—the earliest age he was eligible—the Athenians elected him a strategos, or general. He was annoyed because of a peace treaty with Sparta, engineered by his older military rival Nicias. The Spartan envoys who negotiated the peace treaty ignored Alcibiades—or least he thought so—and this irritated him because he held a political job that meant he was supposed to look after Spartan interests in Athens. When Nicias brokered the peace deal, it was after 10 years of devastating war that was no good for either side. Had no one rocked the boat, the peace might have continued indefinitely. But Alcibiades was nothing if not an inveterate boat-rocker.

When Spartan officials came to negotiate finer points of the treaty, Alcibiades got to them before they could have a formal meeting with anyone in charge. They'd told Nicias they came with complete power to negotiate on behalf of Sparta. Alcibiades convinced them to tell the Athenian assembly, however, that they did not have such powers. He convinced them that if they admitted it, Nicias would extract too much from them. When Nicias arranged the big meeting, the Spartans said they didn't have power to negotiate without confirming anything with the kings of Sparta. This was a huge embarrassment for Nicias, but Alcibiades stood and pretended to be appalled, even though the whole thing was his idea. Plenty of those in-the-know realized this, but the democratic "mob" didn't. The Spartans were shouted down and the whole peace process ground to a halt. Alcibiades arranged an anti-Spartan alliance with some other important cities. This would have been bad enough, but not for Alcibiades. He had to take things a step farther—as it turned out, a step too far.

For many years, Athenians had secretly intended to invade Sicily, slipping in a few troops at a time to help anyone who said the city of Syracuse was oppressing them (there are lots of reasons for this, but it was basically because Syracuse was founded by Corinth and Athenians didn't care for Corinth). After the peace treaty fell apart, Alcibiades whipped the Athenian assembly into an uproar of bellicose excitement when a city called Segesta in Sicily asked for help against Syracuse. Rather than just send a few more soldiers, Alcibiades argued, why not invade wholesale? Once Sicily was taken, Athens could use it as a base to conquer Italy and Carthage. Indeed, had his plan succeeded, the Roman Empire might never have risen. Nicias warned that it was a terrible idea and they'd need lots more men and ships. This backfired, because Alcibiades had gotten them so worked up, they immediately gave Nicias everything he said they'd need and put him in charge with Alcibiades and a third guy, Lomachus, who was the military equivalent of lukewarm water, the "swing vote" between any disagreement between the other two generals.

But the expedition was a catastrophic failure, and the seeds of that failure were sown before anyone left. Shortly before the expedition was to set sail, someone crept around Athens in the middle of the night and, as polite historians like to say, "defaced" the herms—that is, garden gnome-like statues of the god Hermes people put in front of their homes for good fortune. What the perpetrator actually did was knock off the huge, erect phalluses of the herms. It was seen as a terrible omen for the coming war. Alcibiadies may not have had anything to do with the so-called "mutilation of the herms," but his enemies accused him of being the ringleader of the vandals. They also accused him of something that probably was true—holding profane, inverted versions of religious rituals at his debauched drinking parties. This was considered a crime against the gods and punishable by death. In the public panic, the mutilation of the herms became mixed up with the religious charges against Alcibiades as some sort of aristocratic conspiracy to destroy democracy.

Alcibiades demanded to be put on trial immediately, before the expedition sailed. But the sailors and soldiers loved him, and authorities were afraid they'd mutiny if Alcibiades was sentenced to death. Alcibiades was well aware of this and counted on it to muscle his way out of trouble. Instead, the assembly sent him out with the fleet, saying they'd recall him later for trial.

So off he went with Nicias, and after some initial successes in Sicily, the Athenians soon suffered setbacks, mostly due to squabbling generals and lack of expected local allies. As Alcibiades was frustrated by Nicias' cautious approach, the Athenians sent a state galley to take him back to Athens for trial. It seems without being there in person, his golden tongue was unable to sway public opinion and his enemies had been busy.

But Alcibiades had no intention of going to trial. Instead, he fled, took a ship, and went directly to his former enemies, the Spartans. He offered to be their adviser in the war against his hometown, saying that he wasn't betraying Athens, but those who were, in his view, illegally and immorally in control of it.

As an advisor he was incredibly successful. He suggested the Spartans send one of their best generals to Sicily to lead the resistance against Athens—which worked. He also suggested the Spartans capture and fortify Decaleia, a position close to Athens, which ended up effectively capturing the Athenians in their own city and devastating the countryside. Meanwhile, Alcibiades impressed the Spartans by sleeping on a hard cot, eating course gruel, and adopting their lifestyle and customs.

But it didn't take long for him to run afoul of the Spartans, too. He seduced the wife of the Spartan king Agis and had a child by her. Agis hadn't had sex with his wife in 10 months, because of an earthquake (apparently he thought abstinence would prevent another). It was obvious to everyone who the father was, and it didn't help that the queen was so besotted with Alcibiades she told everyone who'd listen that was the baby's real name. Also, despite his early adoption of a Spartan existence, he backslid into his old ways, and offended the conservative community with his arrogant bearing and extravagant lifestyle. So once again, Alcibiades fled.

This time, he went to Greece's ancient enemy, the Persian Empire, specifically a satrap named Tissaphernes, who was himself a cruel, miserable piece of work. The Persian Empire had been giving aid to Sparta for the construction of a navy to rival Athens (the war had worked out so far that Athens couldn't beat Sparta on land, and Sparta couldn't beat Athens at sea). Alcibiades advised Tissaphernes to stay on friendly terms with both Sparta and Athens. Let them wear each other out, he said, then move in and mop up later.

Meanwhile, Alcibiades began to rival even the decadent Persian nobility with his over-the-top pomp. As he became a favorite of Tissaphernes, he simultaneously contacted the Athenians. He told them he was in a position to arrange an alliance between Athens and the Persian Empire—but that things would have to change at home, for the Persians viewed Greek-style democracy as an abomination (as did many of the Greek cities arrayed against Athens). He sent his friend Peisandros to Athens, with instructions to round up the aristocrats and stage a coup d'etat. It was successful almost overnight, and established an oligarchy called the 400, who claimed to represent a secret group of 5,000. Meanwhile, the Athenian navy, stationed at the island of Samos, rejected the new government and vowed to restore the democracy. Irony of ironies, they elected Alcibiades to lead them. He did well at this job, leading the fleet to an important and morale-boosting victory over the Spartans at sea, defeating the Persian satrap Pharnabazos, and conquering Byzantium. He was then captured by Tissaphernes, who wanted to distance himself from him, but escaped from prison after only 30 days. He told everyone that Tissaphernes was party to his escape, which ensured that no one trusted Tissaphernes, either.

And so the fickle Athenians invited him back, having ousted the 400 that rebelled at his instigation in the first place. He returned to Athens as a hero, and was named strategos aotokrater, which made him in charge of all other generals (the only time in the city's history this occurs). He quashed a few minor rebellions, then left to fight in northern Ionia. He left his helmsman, Antiochus, in charge of the navy at Samos. During his absence, the Spartans attacked and defeated the Athenian navy. He was recalled as strategos and officially reprimanded for negligence. He feared more was coming, so once again, he left Athens and took refuge in distant Thrace, where he had earlier fortified an estate. He hired mercenaries and attacked free Thracians who acknowledged no king, amassing a huge fortune.

The Spartans lost no time in following up their victory, and eventually destroyed all but eight ships of the Athenian navy, took over Athens itself, and destroyed its defensive walls. Much in fear of the Spartans, Alcibiades was obliged to take refuge with the Persian satrap Pharabazus—the very one he'd defeated a few years earlier. But the Spartans decided that their victory could never be complete or permanent as long as Alcibiades lived, so the Spartans issued an order to their general Lysander, who was chiefly responsible for their victories, to assassinate Alcibiades.

Word was sent to Pharnabazus, who delegated the assassination to his brother and uncle. Alcibiades was living in a village in Phrygia with one of his mistresses. His assassins set fire to his house. Waking, he threw heaps of clothes and furniture on the fire to stifle the flames, then took his sword and dashed straight through a wall of fire to attack his besiegers. In awe of him once they saw him in person, the attackers fell back and pelted him with javelins from a distance. He died, and his mistress buried him there in Phrygia.

Thus ends the tale of Alcibiades, perhaps the most notorious figure in the Greek world.

This guy once strangled a parrot for speaking French. The poor bastard was the result of centuries of incest, making him—through no fault of his own—one of history's worst rulers.

KING CARLOS II
OF SPAIN

It really wasn't his fault he was a jackass. After all, his parents were uncle and niece, and his family was so inbred over the century before he was born that, while he had eight great-grandparents like the rest of us, he technically only had three (I'll let you figure that one out). At any rate, he was deformed, insane, and utterly incompetent. Whatever he was, he was born to fail: he was King Carlos II of Spain, Jackass of History.

The Habsburgs were a powerful noble family that controlled vast swaths of what would later become Austria, Germany, and Hungary, as well as Spain. To maintain their power, they made a habit of practicing what one commentator called "extreme consanguinity." Routinely, they'd marry uncles to neices, but also first cousins. This ensured no outsiders penetrated the bloodline, but it led to very serious problems—mostly madness and physical deformity. By the time they got to Carlos II, the last male heir of the Spanish Habsburgs, it was clear that their gene pool was polluted beyond repair.

Let me be clear—I would never make fun of anyone or judge someone for having physical and mental deformities. That being said, Carlos II was so ill-educated and over-indulged that instead of being a bit clumsy and dim-witted, he was made by others into an effectively mentally retarded cripple. He was also insane, by any measure, subject to nervous fits, seizures, and violent outbursts. Not that anyone needed to fear him physically: Carlos was, in the words of a French ambassador, "literally sickening to look upon." His head was so overlarge that he could not hold it up on his spindly neck. He had such a pronounced underbite—technically speaking, "prognathism," which was a Habsburg trait but was especially bad in Carlos' case—that he could barely chew food. His tongue was so large that people could barely understand him when he spoke. He didn't speak until he was almost five years old, in fact, and was breast-fed until he was either five or nine (sources vary). He didn't walk until he was eight years old, and rarely left his bed until he was 10 years old. Carlos lived his entire life in a state of constant pain. He couldn't ride a horse or in a carriage without violently vomiting. His doting but domineering mother, herself the result of inbreeding, thought it unecessary to educate her child. All she was interested in was keeping him alive and managing to breed him.

His father, Philip IV of Spain, died when Carlos was only three years old in 1665. His mother, Mari Anna of Austria, became Regent to rule in his stead until he reached 14 (the age of legal adulthood). She did so with a variety of helpers, known as "The Favorites," who were chosen less for their statecraft and fiscal know-how than their dancing and courting skills. One of the worst was Nithard, the Grand Inquisitor in charge of the Spanish Inquisition, which was so powerful as to be able to ignore the rulings of kings. Nithard became the de facto ruler of Spain.

Carlos had inherited a war with Portugal, over the
thorny issue of whether Portugal should have the right
to rule itself. With trouble brewing elsewhere, Nithard
ended this at a high price—Spain lost the crown of
Portugal. Almost immediately, trouble started with
France over lands properly belonging to Belgians and
Dutch—the so-called "Spanish Netherlands"—but
coveted by both Spain and France for the previous
generation. This, too, Nithard ended, resulting in
humiliating losses for Spain.

In fact, the Spanish Empire—once the most powerful
in the world—had been in decline since the 1640s.
Even a great king would have faced a challenge to get
things back on track. With enfeebled Carlos at the helm,
turned this way and that by various court factions, the
once-great nation-state was doomed. The economy was
terrible. Mass hunger was a national emergency. The
monarchy had almost no control over provincial lords.
The nation's finances were in a constant state of crisis.
The court was the center of intrigues and conspiracies
between the pro-France and pro-Austria factions. When
anyone paid attention to Carlos at all, it was to indulge
him in two of his favorite pasttimes—shooting his
gun and counting things, which gave him inordinate
pleasure. He was so over-indulged that he was not
required to clean himself and his half-brother, Juan,
wrote that he was obliged to cover his nose any time
he saw Carlos, and reported that he himself often felt
compelled to comb Carlos' hair. But most of the time,
people just ignored him.

When he turned 14, he was supposed to take control,
but his mother would not allow it, and forced him
to sign a document saying he was not physically or
mentally able to rule—after which, it is said, he burst

from the room in tears and fell down some stairs. Carlos normally had trouble walking, and he was carried most places, even as an adult. This was partly because he was treated as an infant until he was 10, and partly because he inherited the extremest possible Habsburg genetic flaw of a long torso and short legs. At any rate, he would not rule, even when legally old enough. His mother loved the taste of power too much.

Nevertheless, Mari Anna was adamant that he marry, and selected a great prize: Marie Louise, niece of the King of France. Apparently when she heard the news, the pretty young teenager was horrified. When the King told her he couldn't have arranged a better marriage for his own daughter, she replied, "but you could have arranged a better marriage for your niece!"

But she tried to do her duty and produce an heir. That was next to impossible, however, with Carlos. He wasn't impotent—court physicians ensured that he could have erections—but they were very infrequent, and he would almost immediately ejaculate. His doctors even checked his underwear regularly because of this, and, seeing signs that he was capable of ejaculation, blamed the marriage's failure to produce an heir solely on Marie. The poor girl fell into a terrible depression, began over-eating, and died when she was 27. It is said she died from appendicitis, from a horseback-riding injury, or—a popular theory—she was poisoned by Mari Anna, her mother-in-law, to clear the way for another marriage. Most likely she died from complications due to obesity and the lack of a will to live.

Carlos was said to be devastated by her death, but let's look at some stories about how he treated her. Perhaps goaded by his mother, he routinely accused Marie's French servants of plotting against him. He went so far as to have her nurse tortured on more than one occasion. Enraged that Marie's pet parrot spoke French, Carlos managed to muster up enough strength to strangle it.

Within a few months, Carlos was married again, this time to Mariana of Neuburg. She was headstrong and dominant—or tried to be—and became a bitter rival of Carlos' mother. Their mutual bitterness and intrigues nearly destroyed the Spanish court. Things got so bad that Carlo's illegitimate half-brother Don Juan Jose—son of Philip IV and an actress—intervened with military force. He exiled Nithard and drove Mari Anna away from Madrid. There were a few back-and-forths as Mari Anna and her new favorite, Fernando de Valenzuela, attempted to restore her power. But by 1678 it was clear that Don Juan was the de facto ruler of Spain.

Despite the fact that Mariana was specifically chosen for her family's fertility, she couldn't fix Carlos' sexual problems, and that marriage, too, was childless.

Meanwhile, Spain was falling apart, as the Inquisition was out of control and most nobles—with a few noteworthy exceptions such as the Count of Oropesa, who fought to reduce the power of the Inquisition and stabilize the currency—were self-serving or incompetent.

Carlos had one problem that was a benefit to those who wanted to manipulate him: he agreed with whoever was in the room with him at the moment. Perhaps this is why he ordered a mass torture-and-burning session by the Inquisition, who publicly tortured some 200 Protestants, Jews, Muslims, and political enemies, burning some two dozen at the stake. Carlos was so impressed he caused a lavish picture-book to be published about the incident.

But later, someone suggested to Carlos that he order an investigation of the Inquisition. It appears to be one of the few court documents he actually signed. But, when the investigation was complete, it proved so damning to the Inquisition that the Grand Inquisitor told Carlos to burn the document. He probably did, because the first thing Carlos' successor did was ask to see it, and no one could find it.

Later in his life, Carlos became convinced that he was possessed. He told a courtier, "People say I am hexed, and I believe it." In fact "The Bewitched" was a popular nickname for Carlos. It didn't help that the Catholic priests who dominated him agreed, and the record shows that several exorcisms were performed on Carlos. He effectively retired, having gone prematurely bald, losing all of his teeth, and somehow going deaf after a "nervous fit" that we lack details about.

His behavior, as if it wasn't strange enough already, got weirder. At one point he ordered that the bodies of all of his immediate ancestors be exhumed so he could look at them. Church records say he "interfered with the corpses." I don't even want to hazard a guess about what that means.

It became obvious to everyone that Carlos would die without an heir. His mother wanted him to leave the throne to his nephew—and he planned to—but that guy died. In his will, Carlos left the crown of Spain to the French Duke of Anjou, even though some Austrian Habsburgs had a better claim. England, the Netherlands, parts of Germany, and other realms were adamantly opposed to this, because the Duke of Anjou was the grandson of Louis XIV of France, the so-called "Sun King." Even though Louis said he wouldn't interfere, no one believed that.

About the most politically significant thing poor Carlos ever did was die. Fearing a power block of Austria, France, and Spain, war broke out and lasted for 13 terrible years. Even as European wars went, it was a bad one, wrecking economies and killing millions, mostly civilians. And in the end, the only result was that the Duke of Anjou became King Philip V of Spain anyway. At least he stuck to it—to this very day, the King of Spain (yeah, there still is one) is his direct descendant.

As for the autopsy, it's disgusting. The report said that his head was "filled with water," that he had hardly any blood in his body, that his heart was the "size of a peppercorn," that his "intestines were rotting and gangrenous" and that he was "one testicle, shrivelled and very black."

There's lots more to tell about Carlos II of Spain - how noblemen used to frighten their daughters into unwanted marriages by threatening to marry the girls to Carlos instead—or rumors of cannibalism and necrophilia that probably weren't true. Carlos became a sort of dark legendary character in Europe, the living proof of T.H. White's later assertion in *The Once and Future King* that the health and character of a King reflects the health and character of his people. As the once-great, widely feared Spanish Empire declined, Carlos was seen as living proof of that.

Frankly, it's easy to feel sorry for the guy. I don't think any of his problems were his fault. He was a jackass, but with loving guidance he might have done better. Some jackasses are born, others are made. While he couldn't do anything about the deficits he was born with, Carlos was his mother's tool, not her joy, and while he wasn't fated to be, the poor bastard is truly a Jackass of History.

He hated Democrats, Catholics, Jews, vaccinations, aluminum pots and pans, and the American Medical Association. He also made millions by claiming he had a cure for cancer.

NORMAN G. BAKER

If anyone in history has given the phrase "alternative medicine" a bad name, it's Norman Glenwood Baker. He was a confidence artist, a showman, an early version of the ubiquitous pissed-off Conservative radio host, and, worst of all, a quack healer who claimed—falsly, of course—to be able to cure cancer. He bilked thousands of patients out of millions of dollars with his fake cancer cure, which contained, among other things, watermelon seeds and carbolic acid.

Baker's father was an inventor who held some 130 patents and ran the Baker Manufacturing Company in Muscatine, Iowa. Young Baker inherited some of this skill, and he dropped out of high school to wander the Midwest as an itinerant machinist. But he saw a magician's vaudeville act one evening, and that changed his life. Smoke and mirrors—illusion—telling lies big enough that everyone would believe them—Baker would become a master of these skills in the coming years. He created a traveling show that featured the psychic "Madame Pearl." There were, in fact, multiple Madame Pearls over the years, and they were usually Baker's mistress. He even married one, though the marriage was quickly annulled (one wonders if Madame Pearl saw that coming in her crystal ball).

After a decade, he tired of this charlatan show and

returned to Muscatine, where, following in his father's footsteps, he invented an air-powered calliaphone that, reportedly, could be heard a quarter of a mile away without amplification. He also ran a mail-order catalog and a fly-by-night correspondence school for artists. But what he was really interested in was radio. By 1925 he convinced his local Chamber of Commerce to sponsor his radio station, KTNT. That stood for "Know The Naked Truth." Even though the station was licensed for only 500 watts, its actual power was 10,000 watts, and it could be heard all across the continental United States. Baker used the platform to spew invective against Democratic presidential candidate Al Smith: not for political reasons, but because Smith was a Catholic. Baker's program would no doubt appeal to fans of Glenn Beck, Rush Limbaugh, and other modern-day jackasses. He was known for anti-Jewish tirades as well. He was rewarded by Republican president Herbert Hoover with a personal endorsement for his hate-rag The Midwest Free Press, which started publishing in 1930.

Baker had another end game in mind for the radio station. In 1929, he publicly denounced the American Medical Association (he called it the Amateur Meat-cutters Association), claiming they had engineered a conspiracy against Baker's discovery of a cure for cancer. Meanwhile, he was also claiming a vast conspiracy of media moguls was preventing his and other independent radio stations from being commercially successful. Baker was always quick to point to a conspiracy. At any rate, despite having no medical training whatsoever, he opened a hospital in Iowa that, Baker claimed, could cure cancer.

In reality, he bought the "cure" from a well-known Kansas City quack. It consisted mostly of carbolic acid, watermelon seeds, corn silk, clover, and water. The acid caused intense pain in the patients who used it, and they were closed off in a special wing of the hospital so that no one could hear their screams. All the while, KTNT was broadcasting tirades against the medical establishment, who it accused of defaming his cancer cure to drive people toward expensive and unnecessary surgeries.

The AMA didn't take this lying down, of course, and they successfully lobbied the Federal government (and the Federal Radio Commission, which was only just starting to regulate broadcasts) to shut down the station. Baker's license was yanked and the station closed in 1931. Without a steady stream of free advertising, the miracle-hospital's business fell off. Baker sued the AMA, but his public attacks on the head of the AMA for the unforgivable crime of being Jewish didn't help his cause, and he lost the case. At the trial, prosecutors broke down the ingredients of his miracle cure and basically proved it was fake.

Somehow, during all this, Baker found time to run—unsuccessfully—for the governorship of Iowa. He later campaigned for U.S. Senate in 1936, again without success.

In the meantime, Baker went to Mexico and opened a radio station just across the border. This way it couldn't be regulated by Federal authorities but he could still broadcast throughout much of North America. None of this was strictly legal even under Mexican law, but a timely bribe of $35,000 to the Mexican government was well-placed, and the new station, XENT, began a blast of advertising for Baker's miracle cancer cure. He was later convicted in U.S. court for exporting gramophone recordings for purposes of broadcast (illegal at the time, though I can't figure out why) but this conviction was overturned when he filed an appeal.

Baker ensured that XENT broadcasted a combination of anti-Semitic, anti-Catholic, anti-government (especially Democratic government) hate speech, ads for his cancer cure, and "hillbilly music." One of those musicians was from Arkansas, and he sang the praises of the city of Eureka Springs.

Baker visited the resort town and found it down on its luck. The massive Crescent Hotel, once the pride of the Ozarks, had fallen into disrepair. Baker purchased it, and was hailed as a hero by almost all the power-brokers in Eureka Springs (the banks, the chamber of commerce, the newspaper).

...and the money started rolling in. At a later trial, Baker was quoted by a witness as saying he could "reap one million dollars out of the suckers in the state." Desperate cancer patients who'd exhausted every other cure flocked to Eureka Springs, and Baker was able to clear about $500,000 a year—and that's in 1930s and 40s dollars. As in his previous facility, he had one wing shut off, so that the screams of the patients injected with carbolic acid couldn't be heard. He even arranged for his patented calliaphone to be installed on the roof to play constantly and drown out the sounds of suffering. The thing is, the carbolic acid actually did eat away tumors: it also ate away everything else. Pain medication was not on offer. This led to a lot of bad vibes in the "hospital" that, today, give the building a reputation as being haunted. When the treatments didn't work (as they inevitably didn't), Baker would blame the patient for not having the proper mental attitude: in short, he said, anyone who *had* cancer must subconsciously *want* cancer.

Of course, no one was ever cured under Baker's care. He never actually claimed to be a doctor, but hired notorious quacks who'd already been convicted in other states. Despite having the goodwill of the city—to whom economic development was more important than morality—Baker certainly didn't believe his own lies. His paranoia testifies to that: his office in Eureka Springs was lined with bullet-proof materials, he had a secret escape from his office that led outside, and he always ensured that he had a submachine gun within easy reach at all times. These peculiarities, along with his penchant for white suits, lavender ties, and even a purple car (purple was his trademark), led many to think of him as merely eccentric, rather than evil.

The rest of the country wasn't so sure. The famous March of Time newsreel from RKO that preceded motion pictures in the cinemas of the day did an investigative piece calling him a quack, and he unsuccessfully sued them.

However, by this time the powers-that-were had determined to shut Baker down one way or the other. The way they did it was to convict him of mail fraud. He sent out hundreds of thousands of brochures through the U.S. Postal Service, claiming to be able to cure cancer and advertising his Eureka Springs facility. He was convicted and spent four years in Federal prison in Leavenworth, Kansas. The Eureka Springs facility closed down. While he was in prison, his Mexican radio station went silent. His partner sold it to Elliott Roosevelt, the son of the president, who owned radio stations in Texas but couldn't get new broadcasting gear because of the war. Roosevelt received highly unusual permission from the government to upgrade a Texas station, and somehow Baker's equipment in Mexico

ended up in Texas, despite this being against the law.
Baker sued, while in prison, claiming Roosevelt had
special treatment. The suit never went anywhere.

When he got out of prison, the first thing Baker tried
to do was re-open his facility, this time back home in
Muscatine where it all started. But the local government
had no intention of letting that happen. Still possessing
a pile of ill-gotten gains, he retired to a three-story
yacht in Miami. Later reports about him focused, in a
self-congratulatory manner, on his increasing girth and
physical deterioration. Baker died of cirrhosis of the
liver in 1958.

Baker's legacy is dubious on two counts. For one, he
knowingly took advantage of desperate cancer patients,
subjected them to cruel and painful treatments, and
bilked them of their savings. He was also one of the first
"shock radio" personalities, paving the way for a whole
class of radio broadcasters who learned from Baker that
hate and anger sell advertising. What's interesting about
Baker's case is that he is one of the first test subjects for
Federal oversight and regulation of mass media.

To this day, the Eureka Springs facility—now re-
opened as a plush, historic hotel (my wife and I visited
there on our honeymoon)—is known as one of the
most haunted places in America, primarily because of
the tales of weird, experimental, inhumane treatments
during Baker's tenure there.

If you want to hear Baker's side of the story, check out
his ghost-written autobiography, *Doctors, Dynamiters,
and Gunmen*. Written in the style of Christian
hagiography about the lives of the saints (weird,
considering how much he hated Catholicism), it tells, in
Baker's words, of his "crusade to save humanity." It was,
Baker said, "the most important book ever written."

Those comments alone, even without the rest of it, would make Norman Baker a Jackass of History.

Unpleasant Trivia...

• King Edward II of England was a great disappointement to his father, his wife, and pretty much everyone else. He was more-or-less openly bisexual. That would probably have been politely ignored if he hadn't showered wealth and political power on his undeserving boyfriends while simultaneously being a terrible king. He made concessions to Robert the Bruce of Scotland that angered his nobles (especially ones with family estates in Scotland). The Scots utterly defeated his army at the Battle of Bannockburn, which was a calamity for the British that is difficult to appreciate the magnitude of today. Humiliated by this, and sick of Edward's fawning over his favorite courtier, Piers Gaveston, the nobles had Piers not-so-secretly assassinated. Meanwhile, Edward's wife, Isabella, had gone off to France, where her brother, King Charles IV, reigned supreme. He was already irritated that Edward II had territories in France that he'd not personally paid homage to Charles for. To be fair, Isabella had been treated shabbily by Edward, who even took her children away from her to be raised by the family of his new boyfriend, Hugh Despenser (who pretty much everyone except Edward saw as a vain, arrogant, and greedy opportunist exploiting his relationship with the king for personal gain). The French and disaffected nobles in England arranged for an attempted coup d'etat, which turned into a prolonged civil war. Eventually Edward was persuaded to abdicate in favor of his son. In the end, Isabella and her lover, an exiled noble, Roger Mortimer, ousted Edward, captured him, and kept him secretly imprisoned in a series of castles. They established themselves as regents for Edward III, who was still a child. No one really knows what happened to Edward, other than that he was said to be terribly mistreated. He died in prison, supposedly of natural causes, but the salacious rumor spread like wildfire that he was murdered with a hot poker in the rectum. As Edward III got older, he deeply resented Mortimer. As a teenager, Edward III proclaimed himself king and had Mortimer executed for treason. Isabella, however, was left off the hook, and she lived to a ripe old age on a royal pension.

ABOUT THE AUTHOR

PHOTO BY JENNY MCANALLY

Seann Conley McAnally has his own small press, Pharaoh Publishing USA, so it was not difficult to find a publisher to release this book. Born in 1972 to a writer father and artist mother, his involvement in the creative arts was perhaps inevitable. For two decades he worked as a journalist, winning a dozen regional awards for feature writing, graphic design and investigative journalism. Today he works as the director of print communications for the world's largest non-academic sorority. He is the award-winning co-author of *Masquerade of Horrors* (with Colin Lee Campbell) and *A Dungeoneer's Guide to Aeronautics* (with Randall Munden), both supplements for fantasy roleplaying games. In his spare time he enjoys making and playing music and games, studying history, and publishing the works of friends, family members and dead people whose relatives forgot to renew their copyrights. He also enjoys writing about himself in the third person.

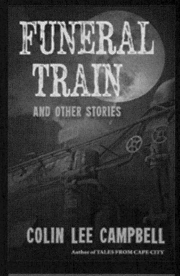

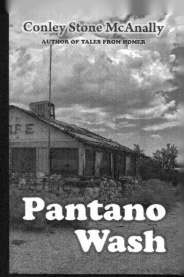
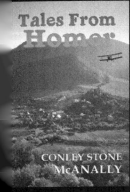

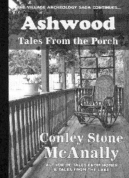
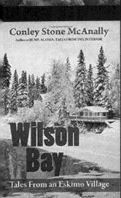

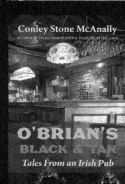

Pharaoh Publishing USA is an indepdendent publisher
of books, music and games in the Heart of America.

We do not accept unsolicited materials.

Contact us at pharaohpublishingusa@gmail.com.

51598255R00104

Made in the USA
Middletown, DE
12 November 2017